WHEN THERE IS
NO OTHER ALTERNATIVE

A SPIRITUAL GUIDE FOR JEWISH COUPLES CONTEMPLATING DIVORCE

*Their Families, the Rabbis Who Counsel Them,
and the Synagogues That Serve Them*

by

Rabbi Sanford Seltzer

UAHC Press
New York

Library of Congress Cataloging-in-Publication Data

Seltzer, Sanford.
    When there is no other alternative : a spiritual guide for Jewish couples
    contemplating divorce, their families, the rabbis who counsel them, and the
    synagogues that serve them / by Sanford Seltzer.
    p. cm.
    Includes bibliographical references.
    ISBN 0-8074-0646-5 (pbk. : alk. paper)
    1. Divorce—Religious aspects—Judaism. I. Title.

    BM713.5 .S45 2000
    296.4'444—dc21

                                                            00-062026

This book is printed on acid-free paper.
Copyright © 2000 by UAHC Press
Manufactured in the United States of America

10 9 8 7 6 5 4 3 2 1

ACKNOWLEDGMENTS

The author gratefully acknowledges the following for permission to reprint previously published material:

CENTRAL CONFERENCE OF AMERICAN RABBIS: Excerpts from *Gates of Prayer for Assemblies,* © 1993, are copyright by Central Conference of American Rabbis and are reproduced by permission; excerpts from *Gates of Prayer: The New Union Prayer Book,* © 1975, are copyright by Central Conference of American Rabbis and are reproduced by permission; and excerpts from *Rabbi's Manual,* © 1988, are copyright by Central Conference of American Rabbis and are reproduced by permission.

HARPER COLLINS: Excerpts from *The Book of Blessings: New Jewish Prayers for Daily Life, the Sabbath, and the New Moon Festival,* by Marcia Falk. Copyright © 1996 by Marcia Lee Falk. Reprinted by permission of Harper Collins.

JEWISH HEALING CENTER: Excerpts from *When The Body Hurts The Soul Still Longs To Sing.* Reprinted by permission of the Jewish Healing Center.

KTAV PUBLISHING HOUSE, INC.: Excerpts from *Jews and Divorce,* edited by Jacob Fried (New York: KTAV, 1968). Reprinted by permission of KTAV Publishing House, Inc.

LILITH MAGAZINE: "Jewish Divorce," by Barbara Bialick. First published in *Lilith,* (Summer 1986); "The New, Improved Jewish Divorce: Hers/His," by Vicki Hollander. First published in *Lilith,* (Summer 1990); and "A Havdalah Ritual for when a Marriage Comes Apart," by Ruth Berger Goldston. First published in *Lilith,* (Spring 1993).

RABBI RAMI M. SHAPIRO: "Interpretive Version: Ahavat Olam," by Rabbi Rami M. Shapiro. Reprinted by permission of Rabbi Rami M. Shapiro.

RABBI SHEILA PELTZ WEINBERG: "Untie" and "Introductions to the Amidah," by Rabbi Sheila Peltz Weinberg. Reprinted by permission of Rabbi Sheila Peltz Weinberg.

iii

CONTENTS

ABBREVIATIONS

B.   Babylonian Talmud

J.   Jerusalem Talmud

M.   Mishnah

Gen.   Genesis

Deut.   Deuteronomy

INTRODUCTION

Jewish couples contemplating divorce, more often than not, feel lost and alone. Many of them want something to read about divorce that deals with issues from a contemporary Jewish perspective and includes some spiritual insights as well. This book has been written with that purpose in mind. Rabbis, family educators, and Jewish family agencies have also sought material that might be helpful to give to couples and to individuals who come to see them during this trying time. Appropriate readings are hard to find, despite the fact that bookstores are filled with how-to books of all kinds about divorce.

Although estimates of the divorce rate among Jews place it somewhat below that of the general population, now presumed to be one in every two marriages, it is sufficiently high to warrant far more attention than it has received. The 1990 National Jewish Population Survey found that a minimum of 172,000 Jewish households in the United States were headed by a single parent, generally the mother, and that at least 200,000 children lived in these homes.[1]

Despite these figures, the limited available bibliography specifically designed for a Jewish audience is mainly concerned with how Jewish law, or halachah, treats divorce. A better understanding of the halachic view of divorce has become increasingly important as the Jewish divorce rate has risen and a good many second marriages involve Jews from diverse backgrounds.

But the complexities of contemporary family situations are such that most have little or no precedent in the Jewish past. By and large these are not being addressed in the current literature. For example, as the rate of interfaith marriage continues to rise, the Jewish status of the children of an intermarried couple after a divorce and the nature of the children's subsequent religious upbringing are growing dilemmas. Yet, concerned families facing this predicament often do not know where to turn for help. As a result, they are prone to handle these issues badly.

Whether one needs a get, a Jewish divorce, and how to go about getting one are another concern. The get has taken on renewed importance in light of the number of remarriages involving couples where one partner is Orthodox or Conservative, and therefore obligated to have a get, and the other is Reform or Jewishly unidentified. In some cases, a person who may not personally be observant will consider a get because, as one woman remarked, "I want to be on the safe side."

Moreover Reform Judaism's recent introduction of a special ritual of separation for divorcing couples called *Seder Preidah* has added yet another dimension to this problem. Many couples are not aware of the existence of this ceremony and of the benefits the ritual can offer them. Others have no idea how to go about arranging to have it done.

Additional issues of ongoing concern include how divorcing couples and their families should conduct themselves regarding children's life-cycle events. What alternatives there may be to litigating a divorce is another question that is often raised.

Gays and lesbians and other Jewish men and women living in a variety of alternate lifestyle situations are confronting domestic conflicts that are similar to those being faced by divorcing couples. They also require guidance and assistance in resolving them.

The standard issues needing resolution in most divorces are spousal maintenance, division of property, and when there are children, custody and child support. All have spiritual aspects, which are too often overlooked and which, if better understood, could make a substantial difference in how these matters are handled.

At first glance, it would appear that there is little available in Jewish tradition from which to draw, other than the highly specific procedures governing the acquisition of a get. It is true that although Judaism developed elaborate and timely rituals for mourning the dead and comforting the bereaved, there is nothing ritually comparable on behalf of the divorced. This is because divorce was addressed primarily as a legal problem and not as a spiritual one. Its emotional price was simply ignored.

Yet Judaism does offer many healing resources. There are selections from the liturgy and any number of gems from the Midrash and Talmud, as well as from Psalms, that can be of great comfort and meaning during this trying time. Also available is a growing library of original and creative rituals and meditations of more recent vintage that have been written by Jewish authors for the purpose of helping men and women who are divorcing. Examples of these will be found throughout this book as well as in the appendix.

Divorce has been compared to experiencing the death of a partner or another loved one. But unlike the mourner who is publicly recognized in the synagogue and for whom there are both formal and informal expressions of concern, support, and sympathy, a person going through a divorce rarely has the benefit of such a network. Not only are formal rituals lacking, but many individuals complain that they are ignored or, what is worse, deliberately avoided by those from whom they expected much more and to whom they had hoped to turn for comfort.

Divorce does take its toll on relationships, as even the most well-intentioned friends are often at a loss about what to either say or do at this time. Others are hesitant to do anything lest they be accused of taking sides. Some do exactly that, embittering the other partner even further.

As a result, people going through a divorce may feel isolated and rejected, convinced that they are alone. They believe that the people they counted on have abandoned them and, what is worse, their synagogues have turned out to be places really meant for those whose marriages are intact and for whom their very presence in the congregation is a threatening reminder that divorce could happen to them too.

One woman described her treatment in the synagogue where she and her former husband had been very active during their marriage, in this way: "Everyone seemed uncomfortable with me at first. They didn't know how to treat me. I sensed that they were unclear about what to do with me, whether to include me in things as if nothing had happened or whether to leave me alone."

A divorced man observed, "When we divorced, I guess I never thought about the synagogue being there for me. I went looking for support for middle aged singles. The temple didn't have anything. I was trying to connect with single parents to share the experience, and the temple didn't especially come through."

Some comments have been even harsher. One disgruntled woman, in recounting her treatment by her former congregation, said, "I sold things to make a bar mitzvah for my son. By the time my second child was ready for Hebrew School, I was on unemployment. The synagogue still wanted $800 in dues."

A confirmand from a divorced household reported, "There was this ongoing problem with names. The staff couldn't get the names right and were annoyed when I mentioned it. And the notes from Sunday school would always say, bring your parents. So I brought them because I felt funny going by myself."

Despite these incidents, many congregations are making concerted efforts to reach out to the divorced and report a decided increase in programming for newly divorced individuals, who until recently had to look to the general community for support. Still, the slow pace in facing up to these concerns is noteworthy. This is especially true given Judaism's historic view of marriage and divorce, which, one might have assumed, would have fostered a more enlightened attitude in the synagogue community.

It is precisely here that Reform Judaism can play a key innovative role, as it has in so many other areas of Jewish life, in reaching out to men and women during this difficult period. "A Statement of Principles for Reform Judaism," which was recently adopted by the Central Conference of American Rabbis (CCAR) at its May 1999 convention in Pittsburgh, has implicitly made such a commitment, even though the divorced and single parents are not specifically mentioned. It declares: "We are an inclusive community, opening doors to Jewish life to people of all ages, to varied kinds of families, to all regardless of their sexual orientation, to *gerim*, those who have converted to Judaism, and to all individuals and families, including the intermarried, who strive to create a Jewish home."[2]

MARRIAGE AND DIVORCE IN JEWISH TRADITION

Judaism has always viewed marriage and the rearing of children as essential for personal gratification, the fulfillment of one's communal obligations and the satisfaction of one's religious duties. The Jewish home was characterized as a *mikdash m'at,* a small sanctuary. Celibacy was rare and frowned upon. The rabbis say that without a wife, a man "remains without good, without a helper, without joy, without a blessing, and without atonement" (B. Y'vamot 63a).[3]

Along with the synagogue, the family was considered the primary means for ensuring both the physical survival and the spiritual welfare of the Jewish people. The many customs and ceremonies practiced in the home such as the rituals for Shabbat and those of the Passover seder are illustrative of the role of the family in safeguarding the transmission of the Jewish heritage from one generation to another. Every family member had a specific role to play in the observance of these occasions as exemplified by the youngest child's recitation of the Four Questions at the seder, the mother's lighting of the Sabbath and Festival candles, and the father's recitation of the *Kiddush,* the blessing over the wine.

The Midrash contains delightful characterizations of home and hearth that emphasize the qualities present in an ideal marital relationship. One story relates that a Roman woman once asked R. Yose bar Halafta what God had been doing since creating the world in six days. "Arranging marriages," came the reply (*Numbers Rabbah* 3:4). In another, God is portrayed as the best man at the wedding of Adam and Eve (*Genesis Rabbah* 18:3).

However, Judaism never entertained any illusions about the tensions associated with family interaction. Neither the biblical editors nor the rabbis lived in an ivory tower. They knew life and its struggles intimately. It is almost as if these lovely rabbinic tales were composed not only to emphasize the potential beauty and joy to be found in a fulfilling marital relationship, but to offset the less palatable failings that were typical of so many marriages in which the Divine Presence was lacking.

The history of Judaism's approach to divorce makes fascinating reading. It can only be touched upon here as it relates to specific topics discussed in these chapters. What must be stressed, and may surprise some readers, is that while divorce was not encouraged, it was nevertheless not forbidden or deemed to be either sinful or unacceptable. It was considered a sad, but occasionally necessary alternative to the continuation of an unhappy relationship. The Talmud puts it most poignantly when it states that when a man divorces the wife of his youth, even the altar weeps (B. *Gittin* 90b).

Judaism's earliest reference to divorce is found in Deut. 24:1, which granted husbands unconditional authority over their wives including the right to divorce them virtually at will. It reads: "If a man takes a wife and possesses her and she fails to please him because he finds something obnoxious about her, he writes her a bill of divorcement, hands it to her, and sends her away from his house."

However cruel and arbitrary this procedure, the fact that a man was required to prepare a formal document of release, prior to divorcing his wife, was in and of itself a modest restraint upon a husband's absolute and capricious authority. The necessity to draft something in writing would also provide the basis for a far more comprehensive and sweeping revision of divorce legislation by the Rabbis, which was far more sympathetic to the plight of women.

A husband's right to divorce his wife at will was forbidden biblically in only two instances. The first was if, after their wedding, he had falsely accused her of having had premarital intercourse with someone else, he could never divorce her (Deut. 22:13). The other was if a man raped a virgin who was not already engaged to someone else, not only was he obligated to marry her, but divorce was also prohibited (Deut. 22:8–9).

In neither instance were the wishes of the young woman considered. In the ancient world, women who were falsely accused of sexual promiscuity or were sexually violated would always bear the stigma of what had happened despite their innocence. Under those conditions, their future marital opportunities were virtually nonexistent. They would always be viewed as "damaged goods."

Biblical law, in effect, delivered a clear message to men that these acts would not be tolerated. They could not be performed with impunity, not because they were ethically wrong, but because the transactional value of the women in question was compromised. Those who were guilty would be obliged to marry the women they had violated, since any potential suitors would now be disinterested in them as wives.

Nor was it at all clear what exactly was meant by the passage in Deuteronomy that allowed a man to divorce his wife if "he finds something obnoxious about her." Later it would provoke a famous talmudic debate over its interpretation. There were those Rabbis who said that its intent was to limit a husband's right to divorce his wife solely to an act of infidelity. The more liberal school of interpreters maintained that a man could divorce his wife for virtually any reason, including finding someone more physically attractive than her or for merely cooking a bad meal.

The passages in Deuteronomy served as the foundation upon which an entire tractate of the Talmud called *Gittin,* or "Bills of Divorcement," was developed. *Gittin* created a comprehensive set of criteria governing divorce, which reduced the degree of male control over divorce and which were far more attentive to women's rights.

These encompassed a detailed presentation of the privileges and obligations of both husbands and wives, the grounds under which either party could seek to divorce the other, the role of the *beit din* (the rabbinical court), and the specifics pertaining to the writing and delivery of a get. (See chapter 7 for a description of these guidelines.)

Later, in a revolutionary decree issued in the year 1000 C.E., Rabbi Gershom of Mayence, the leading rabbinic authority of his day, abolished the male right of polygamy for Jews living in Europe as well as the freedom of a husband to divorce his wife at will. The edict stated: "To assimilate the right of the woman to the right of the man, it is ordained that even as the man does not put away his wife except of his own free will, so shall the woman not be put away except by her own consent."[4]

In effect, women now had the basis for negotiating many of the conditions, particularly the financial ones, attendant to a divorce and were no longer wholly at the mercy of their husbands. By banning polygamy, the decree hoped to elevate the importance of monogamy so that couples would enjoy a new mutuality and wholeness in their relationship.

Although polygamy and concubinage were quite common during the biblical period, the Rabbis were never comfortable with either of them. Their discomfort is reflected in their description of them as among the causes of the Flood: "R. Azariah said in the name of R. Judah that this is what men of the generation of the Flood were doing: One would take two wives, one for procreation and one for sex. The one for procreation would be willing to sit like a widow for a lifetime; the one for sex would be given a sterilizing potion to drink, and she would sit before him like a prostitute" (*Genesis Rabbah* 23:2).

Subsequent codes of Jewish law elaborated upon talmudic decisions and were surprisingly sensitive to the concerns of Jewish women. A case in point is a fourteenth-century dispute in which a rabbinical court was asked to rule on a wife's demand that her husband either stop his compulsive gambling, which was rapidly eroding the family's assets, or give her a divorce. The court responded by noting: "If we can compel a man to divorce his wife on a complaint that he has chronically bad breath, how much more so can the marriage bond be severed for a reason affecting life itself."

In a second instance, a distraught husband came before a rabbinical court with the following dilemma: He had taken an oath to emigrate from Spain to Palestine. His pregnant wife was refusing to go with him. Was he not compelled, he asked, to now divorce her so as not to violate the oath he had taken? The court ruled that whatever the moral questions raised by breaking an oath, the welfare of one's wife took precedence and therefore his first obligation was to her.[5]

Despite all of the reforms instituted over the centuries, Jewish law never accorded Jewish women full parity in suing for divorce. Men still retained the unilateral right to initiate a divorce proceeding. Women could only appeal to their husband's generosity or turn in frustration to the *beit din* to pressure their husbands on their behalf. As we shall see, this inequity continues to pose specific problems for those Jewish women who want an Orthodox get today.

Although the present concern over the high divorce rate among American Jews is fully justified, it needs to be understood from the perspective of Jewish history and a religious value system that made allowance for it. Not only did

Judaism make provision for divorce from the biblical period onward, in the middle ages a primary source of rabbinic income was derived from the granting of the get, an indication that divorce was not uncommon in the Jewish community. "Divorced girls," writes one author, "particularly those whose marriages were of short duration, easily remarried for divorce carried no stigma with it."[6] The same would not hold true for older women, whose chances of remarriage were quite slim.

It also bears mentioning that sociological studies of Jewish divorce rates in various European countries before World War II show that they were consistently higher than those of their non-Jewish neighbors. While these statistics may be attributable to the fact that most of the Jewish communities studied were located in countries with large Catholic populations, they underscore Judiasm's acceptance of divorce as an alternative to marital dysfunction.[7]

Patterns of divorce among Jewish immigrants who came to these shores from Eastern Europe at the turn of the nineteenth and the early years of the twentieth century are equally telling. While many an unhappy marriage that had been prearranged in Europe was formally dissolved upon the couple's arrival in the United States in a court of civil law, an all too common ending was the disappearance of the husband, who abandoned the family.

Ads in the Yiddish newspapers of the day placed by frantic wives still make painful reading. "Max," one letter begins, "you lived with me for six years, during which time I bore you four children, and then you left me. Of the four children, only two remain, but you have made them orphans. Have you no pity for your own flesh and blood? Who will bring them up? Who will support us? Be advised that in several days, I am leaving with my two living orphans for Russia." It is signed, "Your Destitute Wife."[8] One newspaper, *The Jewish Forward,* even created a special column for the purpose of tracing these men. It was called the "Gallery of Missing Husbands." Whenever possible, the men's pictures were also shown.[9]

THE SYNAGOGUE AND
THE DIVORCED FAMILY

This abbreviated summary of the Jewish view of divorce will hopefully help reduce the feelings of inferiority and self-doubt that so many divorced persons have about themselves, feelings that are often reinforced by the reactions of certain friends and acquaintances. It would also appear that they may have been stigmatized by the ambivalent response of synagogues to them.

A few examples may be illustrative. While some congregations report that as many as a third of all children enrolled in the religious school are from divorced-parent households, the topic of divorce is usually absent from the curriculum. Textbooks avoid it. Lesson plans ignore it, and teachers are uneasy about it.

In more than a few cases, the school administration has also not paid any heed to the special needs of these households. Religious school enrollment forms do not ask for the names and addresses of both the custodial and the noncustodial parent. Mailings about the child's progress or calendars listing the dates of parent-teacher association meetings and school assemblies are not sent to both parents.

Any number of divorced parents, usually fathers, have expressed their anger to me about the discomfort and even humiliation of having to call the religious school and ask to be put on the mailing list. Finally having done so, their request was met by the school office with a less than wholehearted willingness to make the change. Ironically, in more than a few cases, the divorce agreement charged the father with the obligation to pay for his ex-wife's synagogue membership and his child's religious school fees.

The problem is not confined to men. A divorced mother complained that rather than taking the time to make up a new addressograph plate for her, the synagogue was sending her mail using the old plate with her ex-husband's name clearly visible, since the office had not done a very good job of erasing it. "Once we got divorced," she said, "I guess they didn't think we were worth the bother to make two new plates."

By and large, the Jewish family is still portrayed in conventional terms in the school curriculum, with descriptions and illustrations in most class materials showing mother, father, and two children assembled at the dinner table on Shabbat eve. Mother lights the Shabbat candles, and father chants the *Kiddush*.

It is a lovely, but wholly unrepresentative depiction of Jewish family life as it really is, in many households. But references to the single-parent family, a situation affecting a sizeable portion of the student body, are few and far between.

The efforts of the synagogue and the religious school to encourage the maintenance of intact and happy families and to strengthen them by stressing positive family values are certainly commendable. If anything, more should be done in this regard. But failing to deal with the subject of divorce in a structured and sensitive context merely contributes to the alienation already felt by youngsters from divorced family households. Many of them either already believe that they already do not belong or are uncertain about their status and their acceptance now that their family of origin has been restructured.

Studies of the effects of divorce on Jewish children present a mixed picture. In one instance, a youngster said, "I thought I made a good bargain with my parents. It was like they were saying, we'll handle the family traditions, you handle the Jewish ones, because my parents aren't all that religious. Then when they got divorced, I must have felt that they broke their end of the agreement, so I could have done one of two things: either break my end of the bargain or keep mine. I decided to keep mine, and now it's definitely for real. I feel that the first and most important thing about me is that I'm Jewish." Positive sentiments such as these need to be encouraged. Ignoring a child's background is not the way to do so.

The reaction to divorce in a second situation is even more illustrative of the synagogue's task. In talking about her family, a girl said, "You didn't have to say anything about us being Jewish. We just were. We were probably more Jewish at home than we were when we went to Temple, which wasn't that often. When my father told me they would probably get divorced, one of the first crazy thoughts I had was, well, you don't have to be Jewish anymore. It was like an agreement I made with my whole family. It made sense because it made sense with the family. But no more. When they got divorced, they said it was alright to forget everything that had to do with the family, and one of those things was being Jewish."[10]

These children as well as their parents need to be reassured that regardless of family structure, their new families, whatever their configuration, are as Jewishly valued as their original families were. They need to be reminded that Shabbat can be celebrated in their homes, as mothers chant the *Kiddush* and fathers kindle the Shabbat candles, and that Judaism does not consider divorced parents or their children to be second class citizens.

The purpose of this book is to make an effort to respond affirmatively to the issues outlined above. Its intent is to try to reassure men and women about to divorce that they will not be forgotten or condemned by the Jewish community and that contrary to their fears and suspicions, the synagogue, which has always been a place of healing and comfort for those in pain, is ready to provide a supportive environment for them.

Although this book is not intended as a manual on the secular aspects of divorce, references to legal facts and trends pertinent to divorce are necessary if the spiritual side is to be examined properly. The legal information and data contained here were generously supplied by my wife, family law attorney and divorce mediator, Rita Pollak. Her suggestions regarding the style and scope of the book were very helpful. Her encouragement at times when, weary and frustrated, I was inclined to abandon this project entirely cannot be conveyed in words.

Over the years, she and I have collaborated as divorce mediators and have encountered every conceivable scenario in our work together. Some of them were frustrating and even tragic. Others implied promising and hopeful outcomes. Regardless of their disposition, they all led us to conclude that while divorce may be unavoidable in certain instances and warranted in others, separating humanely and, if at all possible, caringly was in the long run the most healthy and mutually beneficial thing to do.

The views presented in this volume are mine alone, the reflections of someone who as a Reform rabbi has counseled many divorcing couples and their families and who as a mediator has agonized with countless men and women who, although wishing to go their separate ways, did not want to destroy each other. Some of their stories, albeit altered to maintain confidentiality, will be shared in the hope that readers will learn from their experiences, the sad, as well as the positive.

A special word of thanks is due to Judge Eileen Shaevel of the Massachusetts Probate Court system for her careful review of the legal citations mentioned in the text as well as to Lois Roisman for sharing transcripts of interviews she conducted with a number of divorced men and women regarding their treatment in synagogues. Lillian Maltzer of blessed memory and Davna Brook, each a past chairperson of the Union of American Hebrew Congregations (UAHC) Committee on the Jewish Family during the years when I was its staff director, deserve credit for urging me to pursue this idea, as do the committee members for whom the problem of divorce in the Jewish community and the lack of any literature from a Reform Jewish perspective had been an ongoing agenda item.

I am indebted as well to Rabbi Gustav Buchdahl for permitting me to read his doctoral dissertation, "Jewish Faith, Identity and Ego Repair after Divorce." His insights were most helpful as I framed my own. Tania Ferond, Melissa Freeman, Beth Kozinn Ayo Akunke, Doris Toabe, and Paula Desrochers were all of enormous assistance in coming to my rescue time after time as I fumbled with the computer in preparing the text. Without them, it would have been next to impossible to complete it.

Persuading couples that there is a Jewish component to divorce and that it is possible to end a marriage without crippling spouses and loved ones is what this book is basically all about. It is written in the belief that even when there is no other alternative, broken hearts can be mended, shattered hopes restored, and new beginnings realized.

1

BEFORE
DIVORCING:
SOME THINGS TO CONSIDER

When all is said and done, only those directly affected can decide whether divorce is the right action to take when a marriage is in trouble. However, persons so inclined would do well to think long and hard before proceeding.

FACTORS CONTRIBUTING TO DIVORCE

Impulsive, naive, or uninformed decisions about divorce can be disastrous. Divorce is often expensive and can be psychologically debilitating. Yet its frequency today in the United States would indicate that these dangers have not been very effective deterrents for any number of reasons.

THE CULTURE OF NARCISSISM

Our culture preaches a steady diet of self-indulgence and instant gratification. The late social thinker and author Christopher Lasch called it a culture of narcissism, meaning that people are encouraged to do their own thing, "to go for it" with little or no thought about a decision's long-term consequences or its effects upon others.

In his book *Habits of the Heart,* Robert Bellah warns that this kind of individualism "seems to be producing a way of life that is neither individually or socially viable."[1] Giving up too quickly rather than working at keeping a marriage going is one of the consequences of this mentality.

Hollywood versions of romance, marriage, and divorce have further eroded the perseverance of couples in dealing with their problems. When people get divorced in the movies, more often than not they still seem to have plenty of money, nice homes, fancy cars, and reasonably adjusted families. New partners are just around the corner. The serious side of a marital breakup is either disregarded or dealt with in a humorous fashion so that its truly painful effects are all but ignored.

At the same time, afternoon soap operas, radio talk shows, and TV interviewers regale audiences with titillating stories and personal testimonials about extramarital adventures. Relationships are essentially trivialized as listeners and viewers buy into this steady diet of pap fed by the mass media.

LIVING LONGER MEANS LIVING LONGER TOGETHER

Ever-increasing life spans mean that in the future, married couples will spend far lengthier periods of time together than ever before, especially after children are grown and out of the house. It is estimated that today the average couple is married for forty-three years until the death of one partner.[2] Since many couples are not prepared for marriages of this duration, they often lack the skills to manage them effectively.

The old joke, I married you for better or for worse, but not for lunch, has real meaning today for a great many couples. This situation may help explain, at least partially, the surge in divorces among couples who have been married for quite a long time. Opportunities for teaching couples how to relate to each other later in a marriage when they have become empty nesters have not had a high priority.

One effort in this regard is the Jewish marriage encounter movement. It has enjoyed much success but needs far greater visibility and support than it has received. Based upon a Catholic model, Jewish encounter is intended for couples who are in stable marriages. Participants spend time in a retreat atmosphere exploring and sharing their feelings and finding ways to enhance their relationship. Jewish marriage encounter can also help detect possible rifts in a marriage before they become serious and disruptive.

While some Jewish family agencies sponsor premarital orientation programs and most rabbis counsel couples at whose weddings they officiate, the time spent in these sessions is generally much too brief and the subject matter handled too superficially to make a real difference. One authority, Howard Markham, director of the Center for Marital and Family Studies at the University of Denver, notes that "premarital patterns can predict divorce with 90% accuracy."[3]

If he is correct, well-planned programs would enable couples to identify troubling issues and face up to them well in advance of their weddings and possibly, when indicated, even decide not to marry. A noteworthy new effort in this regard is a five-week orientation to be offered by the Massachusetts Board of

Rabbis, a voluntary association of rabbis from all branches of Judaism, in cooperation with the Hebrew College of Boston, entitled "Making Our New Marriage Work."

The course has been designed to discuss the following issues: (1) Family Legacies That We Bring to Our Marriage, (2) Issues That Challenge Couples in Contemporary Society, (3) Strengthening the Couple Connection, (4) How Jewish Values Contribute to Marriage and Family Life, and (5) Techniques of Effective Communication and Conflict Resolution.

The program is totally optional, and there is no way of knowing how many couples will avail themselves of this opportunity. But it marks an important milestone in community awareness that something should be done to assist Jewish couples in preparing for the complexities of married life.

FEELING THE PRESSURE TO MARRY

Some couples choose to marry even after recognizing that there are serious problems in their relationship. Sometimes the pressures to go ahead may feel so insurmountable that the marriage takes place even though the parties know it is not advisable to do so.

One divorced woman, in recalling the wedding she should have cancelled twenty years earlier, said, "I knew in my heart that it wasn't going to work, but I kept hoping for the best. I simply was afraid to start the whole dating process all over again. All of my friends were getting married, and I didn't want to be left out."

A couple, who ultimately divorced, said that two weeks before their marriage they had decided to cancel the wedding and felt very good about the decision. But upon going to the bride's parents' home, the pile of wedding gifts, not to mention the sight of the bride's mother lying on the living room sofa with an ice pack on her head after hearing the news of their intentions, made them feel that they had no choice but to go through with the ceremony.

DUAL-CAREER FAMILIES

The emergence of the dual-career family is another phenomenon that has contributed to the current incidence of divorce. It has enabled both partners to make new friends and enjoy a variety of social and professional contacts. Often these exclude their mates and require one or both of them to spend periods of time away from home on a fairly regular basis. As new connections are established, sexual temptations may also increase.

The prospect of being sexually intimate with someone else minus the cares and pressures attendant to a marriage can indeed be tantalizing. Articles that speak of the potential benefits of extramarital liaisons to strengthen faltering relationships only exacerbate existing dissatisfactions and help rationalize behavior that deep down those involved know can only be destructive.

When professional obligations demand these absences, couples need to explore ways and means of spending quality time together. Helping them do so is another project that synagogues might well undertake. Since many congregations already sponsor couples groups, the topic of dual-career families is one that might well be on its program agenda. Jewish marriage encounter should also be encouraged.

THE IMPACT OF NO-FAULT DIVORCE

No-fault divorce may have unwittingly also contributed to the mounting divorce rate. It was originally introduced for the purpose of liberalizing archaic divorce laws that had made it impossible in most jurisdictions to end a marriage for any reasons other than adultery or allegations of cruel and abusive treatment. When neither was the case, couples had little choice but to stay together in loveless marriages. The only other alternative was for one party to essentially lie either about the other's alleged infidelity or brutality.

Courts had no choice but to also participate in this unhappy charade. No-fault divorce eliminated the often sleazy atmosphere in which divorce proceedings were formerly conducted. It recognized that no matter how hard they may have worked at their relationships, couples could and did grow apart and should not be coerced into staying together permanently.

Some of no-fault's more subtle consequences, most notably that it would become criticized for being another reason for the American cultural pattern of catering to the whims of the moment, were not foreseen. As a result, some couples have naively assumed that one could simply walk away from a marriage without any liability, be it emotional or financial. Only when it was too late did they discover this to be a wholly unrealistic expectation.

SAVING YOUR MARRIAGE

All of these forces have combined to transform the religious ideal of marriage. Once intended as a serious commitment to be severed only as a last resort, it is now seen as a time-limited way of relating, one that can be easily terminated.

Every opportunity to save a marriage should be explored before resorting to divorce. These include talking about problems with your partner, meeting with your rabbi, and working with a trained marriage therapist. None of these steps is easy. Each has its own complications, and to be honest, all may fail.

TALKING WITH YOUR PARTNER

There are times when even the words "Let's talk" may be heard by one partner as a demand or, even worse, as an accusation that whatever is wrong is their fault. In such circumstances, the familiar reply is, "I'm satisfied with things the way they are" or "It's your problem; you solve it."

Tensions may have been building for a very long time regarding any number of issues. If the pattern in a relationship has been to rarely share feelings, efforts to talk now may be even harder.

If one partner wants the divorce more than the other and has said as much, it tends to create a situation in which the other partner may become even less willing to engage in a frank give-and-take, in the belief that it will do no good.

Beth and Marvin, a couple whom I had known socially for some years, come to mind. Even on the surface, their relationship was such that people often wondered what it was that they saw in each other. They seemed to share very little and never displayed any affection toward one another in public. One day Beth came to my office unannounced and poured her heart out.

She told me that whenever she tried to talk to Marvin about their problems, he simply refused to listen. Things had gone from bad to worse. Now he was spending more and more time in front of the television set at night, and they were not communicating at all.

Although they still slept in the same bed, they had not been intimate for months. She acknowledged that they had both come from families where being open and direct was simply not done. That relationship style had seemingly worked for both of their parents and for Marvin, but it was no longer working for her.

In desperation, she had gone to see an attorney to get information about divorce. When she told Marvin, his reaction was defensive. Rather than hearing the news as an appeal that they could not go on as they had any longer and that they needed to do something about their problems before it was too late, he heard it as a declaration that the marriage was over. Efforts to convince him otherwise were futile. Beth's plea was a cry for help. Sadly, it fell on deaf ears.

MEETING WITH YOUR RABBI

Going to one's rabbi with a personal problem is never easy. Talking about marital problems and the possibility of divorce may be even harder if the couple feel that the rabbi is not open to such topics or will be judgmental about them. There is no way of knowing what a rabbi's views of divorce are unless the subject has been part of the synagogue's agenda and the rabbi has spoken on the topic from the pulpit or at an adult education forum.

One wonders how many rabbinic search committees have ever posed the question when interviewing a new rabbi for their pulpit. A rabbi's reply might well be considered as important as answers about prayer, Jewish education, the intermarried, and other criteria the committee has established for rabbinic leadership. The increased incidence of divorce among rabbis, cantors, and other synagogue professionals has hopefully resulted in a new openness about the subject, which admittedly may not always have been the case.

It was not that long ago that a rabbi who was divorced would have either voluntarily resigned from his pulpit or would have been formally terminated by the congregation's board of trustees. By and large, neither occurs any longer unless there has been a public scandal attendant to the breakup of the marriage. Congregations are now recognizing that marital disharmony can affect any relationship, regardless of one's role or position, and that understanding and compassion are far more appropriate responses than condemnation.

Rabbis can be helpful in providing a safe haven for couples and individuals to air grievances, gain perspective, and share their concerns. Rabbis need to be careful lest, in their desire to be helpful, they go beyond what their skills and abilities dictate. They need to know when it is time to refer the couple to a therapist or an attorney. Taking on this responsibility is not something all rabbis are ready to do. There may even be occasions when negative attitudes about divorce interfere with a rabbi's possible helpfulness.

One husband voiced his rage and frustration after listening to a Rosh HaShanah sermon on the horrendous effects of divorce upon children and the rabbi's stern admonition that couples who divorce are guilty of something akin to child abuse. The man and his wife had planned to meet with the rabbi after the High Holy Days to share their anguish with him. The sermon put an end to that idea.

On the other hand, another couple spoke of how caring their rabbi had been when they talked with her about divorcing. She spent hours with them and made them feel that no matter what they did, they would always be welcome in the synagogue and that her door would be open to them, either together or individually.

When a rabbi's guidance, however beneficial, is insufficient, or when the couple's problems are beyond the rabbi's competence as a pastoral counselor, it may be time to see a therapist.

WORKING WITH A THERAPIST

Therapy has complications of its own. When asked about therapy, some divorcing couples will reply that they saw someone a few times and then stopped going "because we weren't getting anywhere." That statement can mean many different things. One is that as buried feelings were uncovered, and the need to face up to them became unavoidable, one or both persons found the process too threatening to continue and had to find some rationale for not doing so.

Stopping therapy after only a few sessions may also be due to impatience over the length of time needed to really get to the heart of the matter. There are no quick answers to problems that may have been building for many years. Couples need to understand that. At other times, one partner will agree to therapy only on the condition that doing so will guarantee the survival of the marriage or will accuse the therapist of being responsible for its breakup.

Setting up preconditions will only ensure failure. Therapy is designed to help persons gain insight into themselves and their relationship, including why they chose one another in the first place. Whether a couple stays together will

9

depend on what use is made of what has been learned about oneself and one's partner and how their personalities mesh.

Another rationale for stopping therapy is its cost. Yet the same couple who may have spent a small fortune on their wedding and their honeymoon will balk at making a similar investment to save their relationship. It is as if they are saying that since therapy may be long and demanding and offers no guarantees, the investment is not worth the gamble.

Even when a marriage cannot be saved, the insights gained from therapy can be very useful in alleviating much of the friction accompanying a divorce. It can also improve family interaction after a divorce and enhance the quality of any subsequent relationships either party has. What remains essential is that couples can honestly say that all alternatives had been exhausted before they went their separate ways.

Judaism's aversion to hasty or expedient divorces is illustrated in this talmu-dic tale: When King David was very old, the Talmud says, he had a young woman named Avishag brought to him to keep him warm. Though he wished to marry her, he could not, since even he, imperial monarch that he was, had reached the limit of his allotment of wives.

In some bewilderment, one rabbinic commentator asked why, if David was permitted to be alone with the woman, he could not have divorced one of his other wives and married her. Because, came the reply, of how painful it would have been for the wife who was rejected (B. *Sanhedrin* 22a).

REMAINING TOGETHER

There are couples who choose to stay together no matter what the emotional cost. Sometimes a form of paralysis sets in, somewhat similar to the inertia of persons who know they shouldn't get married but do so anyway. The fear of loneliness, of losing the familiar, is simply too threatening.

One woman whose marriage was in shambles said to me, "At least I know what I've got with him, despite it all." Couples who do this live essentially separate lives, preserving the fiction of a marriage for public consumption. There may well be a verbal agreement to do just that, including an understanding that each partner is free to pursue other relationships provided that they are undertaken with discretion.

Other couples remain married, they say, because of what a divorce would do to their children. There is a midrash that when Jacob learned how Leah had deceived him at their wedding, he made up his mind to divorce her. But after God had blessed her with children, he reconsidered, saying, "Shall I divorce the mother of these children?" (*Genesis Rabbah* 11:2).

It is a tender thought and should not be dismissed lightly. Divorce can be and often is very damaging for children. It needs to be examined, however, in the light of the terrible family conflicts that are so graphically depicted in the Bible, of which the story of Jacob, his wives, and his children is a prime example. When families are in such turmoil, divorce may be the lesser of a series of unhappy alternatives.

Others may decide to delay a divorce until they feel that their children are old enough to cope with the strains of family upheaval. It is difficult, if not impossible, to know what exactly is a "good time" to divorce when children are involved. They inevitably pay a price for a family's dysfunction, regardless of age and whether a couple stays together or divorces.

Growing up in an environment of marital pretense is hardly conducive to a child's well-being. Children are very perceptive and soon recognize that things are not as they should be between their parents. The lack of any meaningful family interaction, the awareness that parents are sleeping in separate bedrooms, prolonged absences by either parent from the home, and gossip about other relationships, all make children's lives tense and unhappy. It also provides them with rather poor models for their own future relationships as adults.

More than one parent has been taken aback by the statement of a grown son or daughter who said, "You and Mom should have broken up a long time ago. It would have saved us all a lot of aggravation."

Breaking a glass at the end of a Jewish wedding ceremony is perhaps the most well-known of all the symbols identified with a Jewish marriage. It is a custom that has numerous interpretations. One is that just as a shattered glass is difficult if not impossible to repair, healing a broken relationship and putting all of the pieces back together again is an enormously difficult task. The glass is symbolic of the fragility of every marriage and of the constant care all relationships require if they are to flourish.

Assuming that all efforts at saving a marriage have failed and a divorce is inevitable, what then? What should couples anticipate? What steps can be taken to help ease the stresses and anxieties accompanying separation? It is to these matters that we now turn.

2 FINDING THE INNER STRENGTH TO GO FORWARD

The setting in which divorce unfolds is one that fosters a variety of conflicting emotions in husbands and wives. Anger and grief, not to speak of some misgivings and more than a little ambivalence are all too common responses.

The physical departure of one partner from the home, usually but not always the husband, adds to the confusion and often evokes a simultaneous sense of relief as well as sorrow. This is so even when the couple has long been aware that the marriage would be ending and thought that they were emotionally ready for this moment.

The scene is similar to that following the death of a loved one after a lengthy illness. No matter how prepared the family thought it was for the inevitable, the actual death still shocks and unsettles them. In both the case of death and divorce, mementos of happier times remain visible in the home. Family photographs, works of art, and decorative pieces bought together are vivid reminders of happier times. Albums, gifts, articles of clothing, all underscore the reality of the loss. There is a strange and eerie quiet in the house.

A major distinction, as has been previously mentioned, is the existence of Jewish personal and communal rituals dealing with death that facilitate the process of grieving in a supportive environment, but that are not provided for those who are divorcing. Furthermore, death is final. Divorce, especially when children are involved, means that couples are still tied to one another and must now restructure their relationship.

It remains necessary to maintain communication in order to meet the demands of daily living. There are parenting schedules to organize, a mortgage to pay, and assets to divide. One partner must find a new place to live, while the other is unsure whether he or she can or should remain in the family home. The home itself may be a source of contention. Should it be sold and when? What is a fair price, and how should the equity be divided?

Given this setting, it is not surprising that men and women who once were lovers become antagonists often locked in a bitter struggle over possessions and about what they believe to be rightfully theirs. Two people who once shared tender and caring moments are now hostile and distrustful.

Ideally, there should be a designated cooling-off period, which would allow the parties some time to adjust to all that has happened, prior to the onset of any negotiations. A recently divorced man confided in me that shortly after moving out of his house, he was returning from a business trip. As the plane landed, he suddenly realized that he was unable to go home to his children as he had done for so many years. Instead he faced the prospect of an empty apartment. It was going to take time to come to terms with this wholly new situation. There was, he said, no one with whom to commiserate.

A woman described her momentary sense of desolation as she opened the closet where her husband's suits had hung for so long and found that it was bare. She burst into tears, she said. "I suddenly identified with the closet," she added. "There was an emptiness inside of me which I simply had not anticipated. The temptation to go to the phone and call him was overwhelming."

On occasion, couples will have prepared an informal agreement between themselves, covering most of their immediate financial and parenting concerns, which is to remain in effect until they are ready to proceed with a divorce or decide to reconcile. These understandings may be either verbal or in writing. But generally the prevailing mood does not allow for such advance planning.

The customs of shivah, *sh'loshim,* and *Kaddish* set aside for mourning following a death are noteworthy. Judaism intends them to help the bereaved adjust to what has taken place and accept the loss that has been suffered. The rituals of grieving provide their own form of healing and enable the survivors, in time, to go on with their lives.

Regrettably, there are no comparable rituals after a separation and before a divorce, even thought the need is just as pressing. Like death, divorce is also a time of radical change and requires innovative thinking. This an opportunity for Reform Judaism to introduce new customs to help fill this void.

For example, an evening service could be held at the homes of either or both parties similar to the minyan conducted for mourners immediately following a death. Appropriate selections from the prayer book could be part of the regular liturgy along with supplemental readings especially created for this purpose.

The following recitation is an example:

> God, You give meaning to our hopes, to our struggles and our strivings. Without You we are lost, our lives empty. And so when all else fails us, we turn to You! In the stillness of the night, when the outer darkness enters the soul; in the press of

the crowd, when we walk alone though yearning for companionship; and when in agony we are bystanders to our own confusion, we look to You for hope and peace.

God, we do not ask for a life of ease, for happiness without alloy. Instead we ask You to teach us to be uncomplaining and unafraid. In our darkness help us to find Your light and in our loneliness to discover the many spirits akin to our own. Give us strength to face life with hope and courage, that even from its discords and conflicts we may draw blessing. Make us understand that life calls us not merely to enjoy the richness of the earth, but to exalt in heights attained after the toil of climbing.[1]

Families in consultation with their rabbi could decide how many of these "services of transition" they wish to conduct and what readings they would prefer. (See the appendix for additional readings and meditations.)

There is no reason why friends and family should not be in one's home nightly, as they are for the mourner. Their presence may be particularly beneficial for the person who has moved out of the family home and is living in completely strange surroundings. The importance of caring friends at a time like this has not been sufficiently emphasized by the synagogue.

There is a rabbinic teaching that a visit to the sick alleviates one-sixtieth of the illness. This applies no less to emotional stress than it does to physical pain. Persons who are divorcing may experience both. Many Reform congregations have what are referred to as "Caring Community Committees," which are on call at a time of death or tragedy in a member family. They visit home or hospital and do whatever possible to ease the family burden. There is no reason why this committee, properly oriented, could not be available at a time of divorce.

Sometimes the situation is aggravated by well-intentioned but misguided friends and relatives who prod the separated spouses into taking immediate adversarial action lest the other party gain the advantage. They may relate "horror stories" they have been told about other divorces or anecdotes from the newspaper that are equally terrible.

More often than not, these tales are untrue, oversimplified, or simply not relevant to the present situation. Unfortunately, as they listen, the spouse's fears and vulnerability get the better of them, and they act impulsively. What might have been a fairly benign process is transformed into an incendiary one. The possibility for a resolution of issues with a minimum of antagonism is undermined by the very persons who profess to care the most for that partner and, sadly, probably do.

As a result, couples are often thrown into a legal struggle at precisely the time when they are the most vulnerable and the least equipped to handle it well. Marshall and Phyllis are a couple that come to mind. Before Marshall moved out, they had agreed that he would be able to see their two children as often as possible and that any discussion of what to do about their house would be deferred for awhile. Neither of them wanted to uproot the children unless it was absolutely necessary. Financial responsibilities were to continue as they were during the marriage.

Marshall felt sufficiently comfortable with the arrangement to delay engaging an attorney until both he and Phyllis had adjusted to being apart. He assumed that she felt the same way, as they spoke often to one another, and she gave no indication that anything was wrong. Then one day, he received official notification from an attorney announcing that he was representing Phyllis and that, among other things, she was seeking to have full ownership of their home conveyed to her as part of the divorce settlement.

When Marshall confronted her, Phyllis responded, "I know what we said, but since then I've talked to a number of my friends whose opinions I respect, and they told me what I ought to do." When Marshall then discovered that Phyllis also wanted to limit his contact with their children, based upon "friendly advice," any intention on his part to be reasonable vanished. "It was now a matter of survival," he said. "I will do whatever I have to do." One can only conjecture how different the outcome might have been if "friends" had not interfered.

UNDERSTANDING THE LEGAL PROCESS

For most people, the emotional fragility accompanying divorce is only intensified by having to confront a new world made up of attorneys, judges, and courtrooms during this period of upheaval. They find it to be a strange realm with a language and mystique of its own. The very reference to the partner seeking the divorce as plaintiff and the mate as defendant in the divorce petition comes as a shock and may be a bitter foretaste of what is in the offing in the days ahead. One angry husband was outraged at being labeled the defendant. It was a description, he said, that made him feel as if he were a murderer rather than someone whose wife was asking for a divorce. His humiliation made him even less willing to be cooperative in reaching a settlement.

The resentments generated by the legal terminology of divorce need some elaboration of their own. However litigious American culture has become in other respects, marriage is still painted in very romantic colors. It is seldom portrayed as a legal contract between two individuals granting each of them privileges and imposing obligations upon them that are enforced by the state. The latter is given little thought amid the excitement over the impending nuptials.

Planning the wedding becomes an all-consuming passion. The couple dutifully comply with the requisite legal formalities of procuring a marriage license by taking blood tests and showing proof of citizenship. Having done so, they quickly return to the far more appealing tasks of planning guest lists, honeymoon sites, and bridal showers.

Consequently, one's psychological readiness to deal with the legal side of marriage is flimsy at best. Since few couples have any real idea of what they are getting into when they say, "I do," it is hardly surprising that even fewer are aware of what it will mean should they decide to say, "I don't."

It is noteworthy that while the spiritual dimensions of a Jewish marriage were always significant, its legal ramifications, as emphasized by its designation as *kinyan,* meaning an act of acquisition of a woman by a man, created a very different mind-set for Jewish couples in past generations as they dealt with the purpose of marriage. While tenderness and caring were certainly expectations, glamour and romance as we understand them were not part of the cultural vocabulary of previous ages.

For example, the most familiar explanation as to why Jewish weddings are not held on the Sabbath is to prevent one joyous event from detracting from another. That was true, but there was an equally pressing reason as well. It was to avoid having a contractual transaction, which is what marriage was, take place on the Sabbath. The requirement of a minyan, a quorum consisting of ten qualified male witnesses, at a wedding confirmed it as a legal as well as a religious act.

The Hebrew vow of commitment recited by the groom to the bride, *"Harei at m'kudeshet li b'tabaat zo k'dat Moshe v'Yisrael,"* is freely translated, "Be thou consecrated unto me with this ring as my wife according to the faith of Moses and Israel." In actuality, the word *m'kudeshet* meant that a woman was set aside exclusively for her husband. She belonged to him sexually and to no one else until he died or until he released her by a get and uttered the words, "Behold you are free for any man" (M. *Yoma* 9:1—3). This did not obviate the hopes for tenderness, caring, love, and companionship by any means. It did underscore the specific legal setting in which a Jewish marriage was formalized.

In our day, this vow is recited by both the bride and the groom in the Reform and Conservative wedding ceremonies and refers to the unique relational bond that a husband and wife are to share after marriage. The intent is not one of ownership or acquisition, but of mutual commitment. It implies both a sexual exclusivity and a special intimacy and partnership that no other relationship can claim.

Marriage becomes a sacred covenant. It is an ideal that is expressed in the rabbinic comment that it is not possible for a man to live without a woman, a woman without a man, and both of them without the presence of the Divine in their midst (J. *B'rachot* 9).

In a modern context, the marriage vow affirms that each partner acknowledges and accepts all of the legal obligations that are inherent in the status of marriage. Jewish couples need to better understand both the legal and the religious components of the marriage ritual and the duties and responsibilities these entail. A brief overview of the historic Jewish view of marriage might well become part of the discussion when a couple meets with the rabbi who will officiate at their wedding.

KEY FACTORS IN THE DIVORCE PROCESS

Individuals beginning the divorce process should be aware of three key principles. The first is that the legal system is not an exact science. It cannot work miracles and does not offer neat, simple, and always fair solutions to profound human problems. Second, there is no courtroom or judge capable of either providing a happy ending to a discordant marriage or always deciding a divorce dispute to either party's full satisfaction.

There are individuals who, having suffered real or imagined grievances during their marital relationship, are convinced that they will most certainly be vindicated and get everything they want in a settlement, once their case is heard. What they fail to consider is that judges, however learned and experienced, are only human. Not only do they enjoy wide discretion in deciding divorce cases, they often differ in their view of the facts and in their reading of the law. As a result, the settlement that is awarded may be a far cry from what either of the parties thought it would or should be. The disappointment may become a further source of frustration and resentment.

The third key principle is the selection of the right advocate. Since divorce ranks among the most important decisions a person will ever make, that choice is critical. Generally, referrals come from friends, family members, therapists, or listings in the phone book. On occasion, someone who has been through a divorce will recommend an attorney. A call to the local bar association is also a good idea.

Regardless of the source of the referral, the following guidelines may be helpful in choosing an attorney.

1. If you have a family lawyer, don't assume that he or she can or should represent you. Family attorneys are often not specialists in divorce law. Even if they are, they may not be impartial, having worked for you or your spouse at one time or another, or may not want to find themselves in the middle of a conflict between people whom they like and admire. Helping with a referral should be the extent of their role.

2. Don't be dazzled or discouraged by the decor of a lawyer's office. Posh surroundings with Oriental rugs and wall hangings are not guarantees that the attorney will represent you well. Similarly, someone whose office is not imposing may be a superb advocate.

3. When interviewing attorneys, ask questions about their views of divorce, biases, experience, concerns about children, and style. Some lawyers are combative by personality and training. Others are more conciliatory and do not favor confrontation. You should be comfortable with whomever will be representing you. Divorce is too important for clients to feel uneasy or ambivalent about their lawyer.

4. The attorney is your representative. Clients, because of their emotional state, are often prone to forget that the attorney works for them, rather than the reverse. There may be times when a lawyer may suggest an action that runs counter to the client's wishes. Such reservations need to be voiced openly and directly and the pros and cons examined thoroughly before agreeing on a course of action.

21

5. Listen carefully to what the attorney tells you. Attorneys often complain that clients refuse to listen when told that what they want may not be attainable. The client may balk when informed that compromise is a good idea or that settling out of court makes more sense than going to trial. Not listening can turn out to be disastrous, although being realistic about one's expectations is not always easy given the emotional climate in which a divorce unfolds.

6. Be completely honest with your attorney. However logical that may sound, clients do not always tell the truth or give their attorneys all of the information and facts that are relevant to their situation. When they do not, they make things more difficult for themselves and handicap the person who is their advocate. Persons who withhold information out of embarrassment or the belief that something is not important should remember that the attorney is there to represent them and not to judge them. The attorney is in the best position to assess what is and what may not be relevant.

7. Divorcing couples often confuse legal and adversarial. The two are not the same. Divorce entails adhering to a process governed by a set of rules and regulations determined by the state in which one resides as well as by certain federal statutes. Complying with them does not require conflict and enmity. Being adversarial or cooperative is a personal decision and not a legal one.

In recent years, efforts have grown on the part of the legal profession and the judiciary to find avenues for minimizing those factors that can make divorce a terribly destructive process, so that marriages can be terminated as fairly and equitably as possible. For Jewish couples contemplating a divorce, these are approaches well worth considering. Foremost among them is mediation.

3 MEDIATING YOUR DIVORCE

Sh'lom bayit, or domestic peace, is one of Judaism's most important and best known maxims. The Talmud illustrates its significance in the following way. In chapter 18 of Genesis, when Sarah is informed that she will bear a child, she responds, "Now that I am withered, am I to have enjoyment with my husband, who is old?" However, when God reports the incident to Abraham, he is told that Sarah declared, "How can I give birth, seeing that I am old?" The Talmud explains the contradiction by saying that there are times when even the Divine may deviate from telling the exact truth in the interests of *sh'lom bayit.* For after all, it would have demeaned Abraham to have impugned his virility (B. *Y'vamot* 65b).

The recognition that a Jewish marriage is a religious covenant and is symbolically a metaphor for the relationship between the Divine and the people of Israel means that bringing it to a conclusion ought to be predicated upon an application of the ideal of *sh'lom bayit.* The latter is often ignored in the aftermath of a divorce, when it may be just as vital as it was during a marriage and, in fact, perhaps even more so.

Where children are involved, the stakes are even higher. How a marriage ends and how parents relate to one another when it is over will have a lasting impact upon a child's behavior and well-being. What this demands is that couples ask themselves, "What should Jewish men and women do and not do at a time like this? Are there spiritual guidelines that we can rely upon?"

Acknowledging that a divorce settlement cannot be negotiated in terms of winners or losers and that compromise and accommodation will have to replace vengeance and control as desired outcomes is critical. For couples who are so inclined, divorce mediation can be an extremely valuable alternative to the standard litigation process. Yet it remains a comparatively unknown and underutilized option for a number of reasons.

One is the litigious nature of American society. Jerrald Auerbach, in his book *Justice without Law,* writes, "Law is our natural religion, lawyers constitute our priesthood: the courtroom is our cathedral where contemporary passion plays are enacted."[1] That mind-set inhibits people from choosing non-adversarial opportunities for settling disputes.

A second factor is the historic treatment of divorce by the American court system. Unlike Jewish law, which treats divorce as a regrettable but sometimes necessary conclusion to a troubled marriage, divorce law in the United States was originally predicated upon the concept of the absolute innocence of one partner and the total guilt of the other in causing the breakdown of the marriage. In many states, for a very long time, the only two grounds for divorce were adultery or abuse.

This presumption was a direct legacy of the classical Christian approach to marriage. The statement of Jesus in the Gospels, "What God hath joined together, let no man tear asunder" (Mark 10:9), and which became the basis for the prohibition of divorce in Roman Catholicism, was incorporated into American divorce law in secularized form.

One legal scholar captured the prevailing mood when he wrote, "When the parties know that they are bound together for life, they will resolve their differences and disagreements and make an effort to get along with each other. If they are able to separate legally on less serious grounds they will make no such effort and immorality will result."[2] It followed from this approach that divorce was often adversarial and extremely punitive.

Vestiges of that philosophy still hold sway in some circles. Given the current divorce rate, there are even calls for a reintroduction of more stringent laws governing the right to a divorce and the repeal of no-fault divorce. Single parents are maligned as saboteurs of family values. Women who work outside of the home are vilified. Advocates of day care and after-school care are suspect. In some religious traditions, women are being told to defer to their husbands as the official head of the household.

But, in general, there is an awareness that marital breakdown is usually not a consequence of the struggle between absolute good and absolute evil, but rather the result of the inability of two decent people to live together any longer in a wholesome environment. This has led to reforms in American divorce law such as shared legal custody and no-fault divorce, as well to new approaches to conflict resolution. One of these is divorce mediation.

Divorce mediation affords couples the opportunity to jointly determine how they will end their marriage. Usually it is not as expensive and takes less time than the more traditional format in which attorneys representing each of the parties negotiate with one another after consulting privately with their respective clients.

Couples who mediate their divorces do so together, with the mediator serving as a neutral facilitator as the issues are defined and all of the viable options are weighed. Mediators come from a variety of professional backgrounds. Some mediators are attorneys. Others may be social workers, financial planners, psychologists, or members of the clergy. Persons interested in mediation should interview prospective mediators carefully, not only checking their credential but ascertaining how comfortable they feel with the mediator before making a choice.

A mediator who is an attorney cannot give legal advice to either party. Attorneys may and do provide general legal information such as explaining the criteria for custody, child support, and alimony, the length of time it takes for a divorce to be finalized, and the required procedures and forms that need to be completed for a divorce to be granted. But this is generally done in the presence of both parties as part of an overall orientation at the outset of a mediation.

Agreements reached in mediation are finalized in a "memorandum of understanding." When signed by both parties and notarized, the memorandum can be a legally binding contract, which is often incorporated into the final judgment of divorce.

Most mediators recommend that their clients consult with an attorney before signing a memorandum of understanding. As a rule, attorneys are not present during a mediation, but they still play an important consultative role. They review the memorandum, ensuring that nothing has been overlooked and that the client is fully aware of the implications of what has been agreed upon during mediation.

Not all attorneys are supportive of the mediation process. Some prefer the more traditional attorney-client relationship. Others believe that while issues of custody and parenting are appropriate for mediation, financial questions and matters of taxes and property are best left to lawyers. Therefore, in selecting an attorney as a consultant, it is important to find someone who is sympathetic to the mediation process. When asked, mediators will often supply a list of appropriate referrals.

Mediation is not a panacea or a guarantor of harmony, anymore than choosing to work with attorneys in the more traditional manner is necessarily a prescription for conflict. *Sh'lom bayit* is achievable in either venue. Unless both parties are willing to abide by what has been negotiated, either effort will have been an exercise in futility. Furthermore, divorce mediation may not be a suitable option for every divorcing couple.

Spousal abuse is a special instance in which mediation may be a more problematic course of action for some couples. The wife may be too intimidated by her husband's past behavior and so fearful of what he might do to her after the mediation that she may be unable to act independently and speak out in her own behalf. Whether mediation should take place in situations in which there are accusations of abuse needs to be determined on a case-by-case basis.

Other situations in which mediation may be counterproductive include those in which there is a total lack of trust between the parties or such intense anger that the possibility of working jointly is not viable.

Mediation functions best when it is voluntary. The greater the reluctance or ambivalence of either party, the less likely a satisfactory outcome. Still, recognizing its value, a growing number of court systems are now requiring divorcing couples to meet with a court-appointed mediator for a minimum number of sessions before proceeding with their divorce.

There are occasions when partners will agree to mediation but will show their ambivalence by their behavior as the mediation proceeds. In one such example, the husband, without any advance notification to the wife or the mediators, had made plans for a lengthy stay in another city and announced that he wished to conduct the mediation by conference call. When asked why he had not told anyone of his intentions at the first mediation session, he only shrugged his shoulders and said that he had not thought it was going to be a problem. When asked by his wife to defer his trip until the mediation was over, he chose to withdraw instead.

In another instance, the wife always seemed to neglect bringing requested documents with her to the meetings or to forget tasks that had been assigned in anticipation of the next session. When these lapses were pointed out, she conceded that initially she was less than enthusiastic about mediation and had agreed to it primarily to please her husband.

She went on to say that during their marriage she had always deferred to his wishes and felt that by agreeing to mediate, she had done the same thing once again. Contrary to her expectations, however, she found mediation to be very helpful. Having gained some insights into her behavior, from then on she was very cooperative.

In a third situation, a client named Alex suddenly announced that he no longer wished to continue the mediation just when it appeared that all of the issues between him and his wife, Olivia, had been worked out and a settlement was imminent. In retrospect, it was evident that being conciliatory was intolerable for him.

For such people, the longer a divorce takes, the better, and the more hostility and the more conflict there is, the more gratifying the experience. Law offices and courtrooms are all too familiar with persons like Alex, who refuse to let go, dragging their children and other family members down with them for as long as they possibly can.

There may be times when mediation is indicated, but the pain of being in the same room together for the purpose of dismantling all that a couple had built and shared is simply too much to endure. The psychological distance from one another provided by the client-lawyer relationship may be a more comfortable option. This was the case with Sol and Caroline, who had been married for over fifteen years when they decided to divorce.

Together they had built a thriving dry-cleaning business. At first they had worked side by side, with Caroline handling the bookkeeping and the paperwork as Sol did the cleaning and ironing in the back room of the store that they had rented. Over the years they had prospered. The divorce was to be friendly, and they had wanted to mediate.

But it was "just too hard," as Caroline put it through her tears at one session, "to sit here and personally tear apart everything it took us so long to put together." She needed the space and the comparative anonymity a divorce lawyer could provide. "It would hurt less that way," she said.

There are occasions when mediation may be a good idea for resolving some, but not all of a couple's disagreements. One couple, Jed and Marsha, agreed that it was pointless to try to settle financial matters. They had been unable to do so during their marriage, and the constant bickering over money had led to their divorce. Mediation had enabled them to answer all of their parenting questions and to divide family possessions with a minimum of rancor. They had a mutual sense of accomplishment for which they were both grateful. When it came to money, however, they preferred to have two attorneys work out the details for them.

On the other hand, Harriet and Phil had come to mediation for the express purpose of finalizing a financial agreement. They had jointly drafted a proposal but wanted to be sure that it was fair and comprehensive. For them, mediation was the right setting for doing so.

Although there is no direct connection between divorce mediation and Judaism, there are precedents in Jewish tradition and Jewish history that are noteworthy. For example, centuries ago, when courts of Jewish law were in existence, the emphasis was upon conciliation, rather than the victory of one party over the other. A ploy used by rabbinic members of the court as a means of discouraging a couple from divorcing was to initially delay the paperwork and tell the couple to come back the following day or week, in the hope that they would reconsider in the interim. If that was not successful, the court would insist upon having the rabbi of the adjacent town also consulted before the divorce was granted.

There were no attorneys to plead the case of the aggrieved. They spoke for themselves. According to Maimonides, "a court which always settles cases by compromise, is praiseworthy."[3]

In the early years of the twentieth century, as large numbers of Jews came to these shores from Eastern Europe, Jewish conciliation courts were organized on the Lower East Side of New York for the purpose of resolving a whole variety of disputes, civil and religious, that were brought before them by members of the k'hillah, as the Jewish community was known. These efforts were particularly effective in the clothing, fur, and millinery industries, which employed large numbers of Jews. A Bureau of Industry was established, which was staffed by full-time mediators, who resolved disputes by mediating them.[4] By and large, the court dockets did not extend to divorce, however.

Today, rabbis are in the unique position of being able to encourage couples considering divorce to avail themselves of the services of a mediator and to impress upon them not only the potential advantages of this form of divorce resolution, but the Jewish precedents for doing so as well.

A new approach to divorce resolution, known as collaborative law, is now being considered by some attorneys. One of its supporters, Rita Pollak, in a paper entitled, "Beyond the Code of Professional Responsibility—Can Spiritual Values Be Our Compass?" used references from the works of Jewish mystics who focus upon the Sparks, or Emanations of the Divine, to make her point. She writes:

> Divorce, uncoupling, shattering the vessel of the family is a dra-
> matic and profound way to disconnect.... Perhaps some people
> are at their worst, because that spark of Divinity has temporar-
> ily been diminished or even extinguished.... Clients certainly
> tell us that it feels like utter despair, hopelessness, loss of love,
> admiration, respect, self esteem, role, home family; it feels like
> hell.... I try to lawyer toward connection, toward resolution....
> If we view the "other side" as somehow wrong, unworthy, weak

or bad, we'll never be able to build connection with them or truly help them or truly help our own client to reconnect to his/her partner in the spirit of resolution. We will not achieve wholeness...repairing the shattered vessel, if we help snuff out the Divine Spark in any person.[5]

Collaborative law is based upon the principle that those involved, clients and attorneys alike, will negotiate a settlement by creative problem solving and will not threaten or engage in litigation to get results. It is a process that reminds one of the methods employed by rabbinical courts in past centuries, even though there is no apparent connection between them.

Part of the agreement entered into by couples who choose this form of conflict resolution contains the following stipulation: "We understand that the process, even with full and honest disclosure, will involve vigorous good faith and negotiation. Each of us will be expected to take a reasoned position in all disputes. Where such positions differ, each of us will be encouraged to use our best efforts to create proposals that meet the fundamental needs of both of us and if necessary to compromise to reach a settlement of all issues. Although each of us may discuss the likely outcome of a litigated result, none of us will use threats of litigation as a way of forcing settlement."[6]

There are no foolproof methods for ending a marriage satisfactorily. Whether a divorce is mediated or negotiated by attorneys, the ultimate outcome will depend upon the integrity and goodwill of the couple and how determined they are to reconnect those Divine sparks that have been scattered. Former spouses bent upon punishing each other will find ample ways of doing so. Persons determined to undermine a divorce agreement will quickly discover how to achieve that goal. Hopefully, rabbis, attorneys, mediators, and loved ones can all be instruments of healing and restoration.

Sample Parenting Schedule in a Memorandum of Understanding

(Name of couple), having determined to divorce, wish to do so in as fair and equitable a manner as possible. Their primary concern is the health and welfare of their child. They have, therefore, entered into this memorandum of understanding.

A. Custody

Both parties agree that they will have shared legal custody of (name of child), thereby being mutually responsible for all legal, medical, educational, and religious aspects of their child's upbringing. It is further agreed that mother will have physical custody of child.

B.   Interaction as Parents

Both parties recognize that in the best interests of their child, they will endeavor to be respectful and civil to one another and will not engage in name calling or other hostile behavior. Neither parent will interfere with the other's parenting prerogatives when child is in their respective care.

C.   Parenting Schedule

Both parties have agreed to the following parenting schedule with the understanding that it is open to modification and revision if mutually agreed upon.

1.   Weekly Arrangements

a.   Child will spend every Wednesday with father, who will be responsible for taking child to school on that day.

b   Child will spend every other weekend with father at his residence. Father will pick child up after school on Friday and take child to religious school on Sunday, where mother will pick child up.

c.   On alternate weekends, child will spend either all day Saturday or Sunday after religious school with father. The specific day and time will be decided by parents.

2.   Holidays

January: Martin Luther King Day—child will be with father unless he notifies mother at least two weeks in advance to the contrary and they agree to alternate arrangements.

February: School vacation—child will be with father on Monday and with mother on Friday. The middle days will be divided between friends and sitters. Costs will be shared equally.

March: No holidays—regular schedule.

April: Spring vacation—child will be with mother.

May: Mother's Day—child will be with mother. Memorial Day weekend—to be determined by both parents two weeks before the holiday.

June: Father's Day—child will be with father.

July: July 4—child will be with father.

August: Child will be at overnight camp. Week before the end of camp and the start of the school year—to be determined.

September: Labor Day weekend—child will be with mother.

October: Columbus Day weekend—child will be with mother.

November: Veterans Day—child will be with father. Thanksgiving—child will be with father on Thanksgiving Day and with mother on the Friday after Thanksgiving Day.

December: School vacation—child will be with father on Monday, Christmas Day, and the day after; mother will make arrangements for the rest of the week. New Year's—child will be with father on New Year's Eve and with mother on New Year's Day.

3. Child's Birthday: The parties have agreed to a joint celebration.

4. Jewish Holidays

Rosh HaShanah: child will be with father.

Yom Kippur: child will be with mother.

Chanukah: child will spend time with both parents with the proviso that father wishes to light candles with child on the first night.

Passover: In the year _____ child will spend Passover with mother. The following year it is agreed that the child will celebrate the first seder with father and the second with mother. After that, parents will alternate seders each year.

Both parties agree that this schedule is subject to renegotiation as circumstances warrant and any changes will be done in good faith.

4 Custody, Child Support Additional Family Matters, and Life-Cycle Events

Divorce is never pleasant. The degree of pain and discomfort it causes increases exponentially when there are other family members to consider. The presence of children, grandparents, and other relatives contributes to a far more emotionally complex process than most people imagine. There are any number of critical decisions affecting the family that need to be made in the course of a divorce and its aftermath, which are reviewed here from a Jewish point of view.

UNDERSTANDING WHAT CUSTODY IS ALL ABOUT

Custody is the legal term pertaining to the process of deciding which parent will have primary responsibility for a child's welfare after a divorce. Perhaps the two greatest fears of divorcing parents are first, that henceforth one's right and even style of parenting may be subject to regulation and scrutiny by the court until children come of age; and second, that a judge will decide the other parent is the more appropriate to be awarded primary custody.

The fear of losing custody has been a compelling reason why some couples stay together in an unhappy marriage, while others engage in bitter disputes during and after a divorce. When custody is contested, courts may appoint a special investigator known as a guardian ad litem (GAL), whose function is to decide in which parent's care a child's future would be better served.

The guardian ad litem will interview both parents, speak to the children, and visit each home in an effort to determine parental fitness. It is not an easy decision to make. For parents, the knowledge that the future nature of their relationship with their children is to be decided by a virtual stranger can be both infuriating and frustrating.

Sometimes parents welcome the "GAL," confident that any objective evaluator will name them as the better parent. In other instances, their attitudes reflect their anxieties over this turn of events. The guardian ad litem then reports the findings to the judge hearing the case, who will make the final determination, but whose decision will be greatly influenced by these recommendations.

CUSTODY IN JEWISH TRADITION

Jewish attitudes regarding custody as found in the Talmud reflect the value systems of the cultures in which Jews lived. It was customary for both boys and girls to live with their mothers until the age of six. At that time, boys often reverted to the custody of their fathers and girls remained with their mothers, who were to instruct them in the various duties connected with homemaking. Later, rabbinical courts, as long as they had the power to do so, awarded custody at their discretion.

A father was obligated to see to his son's ritual circumcision, *pidyon haben* if he was a firstborn, bar mitzvah, and study of Torah and to teach him a trade and how to swim. He was also responsible for making provisions for an early marriage for all of his children.[1] On the other hand, a father was not responsible for the maintenance of a minor daughter. In fact, according to the Mishnah, he had no legal obligation to either feed or clothe her.

Yet, when it was time for her to be married, a father was required to provide an appropriate trousseau. This seeming contradiction between the neglect of a child's food and clothing and supplying a dowry for her marriage had more to do with the father's self-image and reputation, in transferring an item of property in good condition, namely a daughter, to a new owner, her husband, than with any concern over the welfare of the girl as a minor child (see M. *K'tubot* 4:6 and 6:5).

It can be argued that a provision for child support, regardless of gender, was implicit in the stipend a husband who divorced his wife was compelled to pay her. The amount as stipulated in the *ketubah*, the marriage contract entered into before the marriage, could be quite substantial and was intended as a means of discouraging husbands from divorcing their wives casually.[2] But the absence of any enlightened approach in Jewish sources to what we refer to as custody is an unfortunate reality.

SHARED LEGAL CUSTODY

The most far-reaching among the changes made by the legal system in determining parental roles after a divorce has been a presumption of shared legal custody. Shared legal custody is now operative in some form in virtually all of the fifty states.

A presumption of shared legal custody provides that both parents will have an equal voice in the resolution of the legal, medical, educational, and religious issues affecting their children. Unless it can be shown conclusively that a child's father is unfit to exercise this opportunity or he asks that it not be accorded him, shared legal custody is now fairly standard. The former practice of granting mothers sole responsibility for their children and of relegating fathers to the role of part-time weekend social director with little ongoing input into a child's life is no longer the norm.

Unless the parents have been awarded shared physical custody, a practice no longer as uncommon as it once was, children continue to have one primary custodial parent, usually but not always the mother, as this precedent has also changed, and one official home address. Critics insisted that any form of shared custody would not work, because parents would not be cooperative. However, experience has shown that there is no necessary correlation between how couples interacted during their marriage and their ability to communicate after it ended, especially when children were involved.

This does not mean that parents always cooperate as well as they might or that all issues are resolved to everyone's mutual satisfaction. There are times when either or both parents may be frustrated by the restrictions imposed upon their freedom of action as a result of sharing legal custody. The primary custodial parent may long for a return to the "good old days" when he or she could make all the decisions about the child's welfare alone.

What has been achieved is that children do not feel deprived of the involvement of either parent in their lives and the father does not consider himself disenfranchised as a parent, but can be an active participant in making decisions regarding his child. This ability affords him a renewed sense of self-esteem, which can benefit everyone, since it is now presumed that the father's attitude toward parenting will be far more positive.

Shared legal custody has raised some new complications, however. One is the necessity to confront a diversity of parenting styles and values. Arguments about television, bedtime, or snacks, which often took place during the marriage and were sources of parental conflict then, are even more likely now to become lightning rods, pushing one parent to criticize the other's judgment.

It is important that parents both acknowledge and convey to their children that these decisions are the prerogative of the parent who is caring for the child at that time. Admittedly that may be easier said than done, since children may tend to exploit these inconsistencies as much as they can. The refrain "But Daddy says" or "Mommy lets us" is all too familiar. Still, while there is always room for discussion, neither parent should interfere with the other's parenting style unless there is a real danger to a child's moral, physical, or emotional well-being.

Myrna and Al were the perfect example of the old adage that opposites attract. They could not have been a more diverse pair in terms of their interests and their outlook on life. A librarian by profession, Myrna loved good books, the symphony, and the art museum, values she had sought to inculcate in their only child, Gordon, now twelve.

Her husband, Al, was a husky six-footer, who worked out daily, played basketball, and couldn't wait for the ski season to begin. He encouraged his son to be athletic and stressed the value of contact sports, including hockey and football. Gordon's physical activities and Myrna's fears of his getting hurt had been a continuous source of conflict between them during their marriage.

It was a matter that she raised at every mediation session, at one point even asking to have their agreement include some language that would limit the boy's freedom to participate in sports. There was no evidence that Gordon was doing anything harmful or dangerous. In fact, as Myrna herself admitted, he enjoyed these activities very much, always wore the right equipment, and took the necessary precautions, something his father was very strict about. Furthermore, he was very cooperative in attending the cultural events she made available when he was with her and seemed to enjoy them as well.

But it was a very hard adjustment for her to make. It would be quite awhile, if ever, before she could accept the fact that Gordon's lifestyle was not something that she would be able to control. Presented with two striking alternatives, he would in time make his own choices.

Shared legal custody may require more contact than one or both parents may desire. One former husband announced that he was looking to buy a house in the neighborhood where the couple had lived when they were married. It was the last thing his ex-wife, who was still in the original family home with their children, wanted. She sensed that it was more a means on his part to deny the end of the marriage and keep tabs on her social life than having anything to do with shared legal custody of their children. When he changed his mind and moved elsewhere, she was visibly relieved.

When parents share legal custody, the need for more frequent communication may also delude the partner who did not want the divorce in the first place into imagining that there is now a possibility of reconciliation. Phone calls and requests that "we get together to talk about the kids," however seemingly legitimate, may be a pretext for other motives.

Unless this sort of behavior is confronted directly, children can be seduced into thinking that parents are seriously considering reconciling, a fantasy that many children indulge in for a very long time. They may ask if Daddy can stay for dinner or even spend the night. The response will need to be clear and direct if matters are not to get out of hand.

Special situations often pose a problem. For one family, it was the father's mail-order business, which he conducted in the basement of their home. The divorce agreement allowed him to continue to use the space after the divorce. During their marriage, he had been accustomed to taking breaks during the day and going upstairs into the kitchen to make coffee, read the paper, go through his mail, and spend some time with the children. He now tended to do the same thing, although it was no longer appropriate. It was a pattern that was extremely hard to break. Finally the situation became so untenable, he moved his office elsewhere.

Whatever the ultimate parenting arrangement, parents should cooperate and draft plans that are attuned to their children's needs and schedules as well as to their own. However creative these may be in theory, their workability will be contingent upon a mutual willingness to abide by them. Both parents' promotion of respect and confidence of the children in the other is an overriding consideration.

Derogatory, belittling, and hostile comments to children about their father or mother can only be destructive, whether it be done in private or when the parents are together. The injunction in the Ten Commandments to honor one's father and mother will ring hollow to children who are constantly harangued by one parent about the other's faults and shortcomings or who are told when they misbehave, "You are just like your father" or "You are just like your mother."

It bears emphasizing that should one parent die, the other, barring exceptional circumstances, will automatically become the sole custodian of the children. If that parent has been disparaged or deliberately kept at bay after the divorce, the children may suffer severe psychological harm now that they will be living with the very person who had been painted in such terrible colors. It is not a healthy scene. Great care should be taken to ensure that it does not occur

Rabbis who familiarize themselves with shared legal custody and its nuances can be of great assistance in reaching out to parents who are ambivalent about what will happen under this arrangement or who just need some general backup and support as the process of children moving between two households begins. Giving attention to this "life-cycle" reality is as important as that given to death and dying, hospital visitation, and other pastoral duties.

PAYING CHILD SUPPORT

The failure of fathers to pay child support has become a national scandal of such proportions that now there are both state and federal laws providing for the arrest and prosecution of so-called deadbeat dads. Susan Faludi, in her book *Backlash: The Undeclared War against American Women*, writes that divorced men are more likely to meet their car payments than their child support payments.[3] While there are instances where the parent liable for child support is the mother, by and large it is still the father who bears this responsibility.

One of the problems with child support is that there are no national standards to determine how much is to be paid or what deductions and other criteria regarding a father's income or a mother's expenses are to be utilized in making that assessment. The formula for child support varies from state to state. The amounts in some states are much higher than in others.

Although the statistics are limited regarding Jewish fathers, many of them are also guilty of either trying to avoid the payment of child support or reducing what they have to pay. A decade ago, one study estimated that 40 percent of Jewish fathers paid no child support at all or contributed less than 10 percent of their income and decreased their payments within three years after a divorce.[4] More recent data about Jewish fathers and their child support payments are not available.

The failure of most Federation surveys of Jewish populations in major American cities to ask the question is a telling commentary on the reluctance to gather information about divorce in the Jewish community. When the little that is known is added to the statistic showing that over 30 percent of all divorced women never remarry, the economic plight of women and children after divorce becomes even more graphic.

It was hoped that legal reforms that afforded men greater access to their children after divorce, such as shared legal custody and liberal parenting opportunities, would reduce the problem of noncompliance. While these have helped, too many fathers continue to avoid their responsibilities. At times, some of them are incredibly thoughtless and destructive in doing so.

One frustrating example is the story of Mark, who with his wife, Tess, had come to mediate their divorce. The couple had three young children, ages five, seven, and eleven. Mark held an executive position in a well-known corporation and earned a sufficient income not only to meet his child support obligations but to allow him to live quite comfortably as well after the divorce.

The mediation had proceeded smoothly. Mark had raised no objections to the amount of child support that was incorporated into the couple's memorandum of understanding. On the day upon which it was to be signed, Mark announced that he had just quit his job. He had not, he said, been happy at the company for a very long time. He was convinced that given his professional credentials, he would be able to find something else equal or superior to the position he had just left, in short order.

There was a moment of stunned silence around the table. Tess stared at Mark in disbelief. Other than Mark's income, the family had few assets to fall back upon. The settlement and the arrangements had been predicated upon Mark's salary. Tess had never worked more than part-time, and the children were all in private school.

Later it was discovered that leaving his job the way he did was Mark's misguided way of forestalling the divorce he had not wanted in the first place. He had taken this drastic step in the mistaken belief that Tess would not go ahead without sufficient income to rely upon. He was wrong. She was now even more determined than ever to end the marriage, whatever the financial problems his behavior had caused.

Fathers tend to confuse the frequency of visitation with their children, regardless of whether it is limited by a judge or based upon their own interest, with the amount of child support they should be paying. One has little to do with the other. Some fathers have threatened to sue their wives for full custody of their children in hopes of pressuring them into accepting a lesser amount of child support.

In some instances, mothers have simply given up the legal battle either because of the delays and the legal costs attendant to pressing the issue or out of fear that fathers who are forced to pay what is the rightful amount of support will harass them and the children in retaliation. As a consequence, they prefer to leave well enough alone.

There are fathers who insist that the burden imposed upon them is unfair in light of the financial responsibilities brought about by a second marriage and another family. But a voluntary decision to remarry does not absolve fathers of their original parental obligations. Starting a second family without regard to the needs of the first is irresponsible.

At other times, fathers withhold child support after claiming that the money is being squandered or not being used for the child but rather for the indulgence of the mother, or because the wife has remarried and her new husband is financially comfortable and able to take care of her and the children. Courts have not been sympathetic to the first argument unless the father provides convincing evidence that verifies that allegation. Until he does, payment should not be withheld. Courts have consistently maintained that the economic well-being of a second husband or his generosity does not absolve the natural father from paying child support.

There are no easy answers to alleviating the financial burdens families face after a divorce. The old adage that two families cannot live as cheaply as one is painfully true. Battles over money merely aggravate matters. Making children the victims of financial struggles is not the way to solve the problem.

There is a Jewish dimension to the obligation of child support that is beautifully conveyed in the following midrash. When the people of Israel stood at Sinai to receive the Torah, God said to them, "Bring me some collateral to guarantee that you will keep its teachings." The people first said, "The prophets will be our collateral." When the offer was rejected, they next offered their ancestors, and this too was not acceptable. At last they said, "Our children will be our collateral." This was accepted, and they received the Torah (B. *Kiddushin* 29b).

Having fulfilled the mitzvah of bearing children and having entered them into the covenant of Israel, it is important that parents remember that the parental bond is stronger than the marital bond and should be honored accordingly. Judaism does not provide a ritual for divorcing one's children.

The dereliction of a parent in failing to pay child support is another matter regarding which the rabbi and the synagogue can be helpful. Sermons, adult education seminars on the contemporary Jewish family and its concerns, and when possible, a meeting with the parent involved are all avenues to be pursued. National Jewish bodies need to be far more outspoken on the subject of child support than they have been in the past.

BAR AND BAT MITZVAH

Nurturing one's child financially is but one aspect of fulfilling the parental role. How parents and other family members relate to one another at life-cycle events, particularly bar and bat mitzvah, is just as crucial.

Bar and bat mitzvah have become the most dominant events in the religious calendar of the American Jewish family. No other occasion has such a powerful hold on the family regardless of their degree of piety or synagogue involvement. No other occasion is so potentially explosive.[5]

For divorced couples and their children, it may also be the most dreaded moment to be confronted since the actual divorce itself. Whatever the extent of their discomfort with one another, divorced parents may have attended parent-teacher association meetings, school plays, and athletic events involving their children with a minimum of anxiety. Even confirmation, primarily because it is a group celebration, may have been uneventful. But the occasion of a bar or bat mitzvah is another matter entirely.

Both partners are uneasy and self-conscious. The prospect of relatives and grandparents from both sides of the family reassembling is not very reassuring. Like it or not, for however brief a time, the original extended family unit has suddenly been reconstructed. If the divorce was antagonistic and accompanied by heated exchanges between family members, this artificial reunion may provoke unpleasant reminders of who said what to whom.

The synagogue setting evokes its own disturbing memories. If the couple were married here, worshiped together, or were active on the temple board or one of its committees, those memories add to the tension. One or both parties may have grown up in the congregation as well. Their child may have been blessed and named by the rabbi at birth as the parents stood side by side on the very pulpit where the child now stands.

To make matters worse, some divorce agreements stipulate that one partner, usually the father, must resign from the congregation. Other agreements are even more extreme. In one divorce mediation, the mother, who taught in the synagogue religious school, insisted that the father of their child not only leave the congregation, but agree never to pick the little girl up at the religious school even during those times when the child was in his care. Instead, the mother was prepared to drive the child to the father's house. Although she finally relented regarding his temple membership, she could not be dissuaded from her insistence that the father never enter the religious school. The father grudgingly complied in order to keep peace.

When a couple's postdivorce relationship is this hostile, cooperation before a bar or bat mitzvah will be no easy matter. There may even be instances when one parent will attempt to prevent the other from participating in the service or from even being present in the synagogue. In response, the latter may threaten an open confrontation or take legal action. Violence is not an impossibility.

If one partner has remarried, he or she may want a stepparent to participate in the ritual. The request is reasonable if that person has played a legitimate role in the child's upbringing. If it is a pretext for hurting the natural parent, it needs to be treated accordingly. When more than one set of parents is involved in the allocation of honors, the procedure will need to be carefully planned.

In one instance, a stepfather who had not entered the bat mitzvah's life until the girl was twelve chose not to participate despite the mother's desire that he do so. He felt that if he did, he would needlessly antagonize the child's father, who, although caring and financially reliable, saw her infrequently because he lived in a distant community. Instead, he chose to sit in the congregation. Later, the natural father made a point of thanking him for his sensitivity and tact.

The increase in the number of blended families in the Jewish community has not only given stepparents a much more prominent role in children's lives than ever before, it has created new opportunities for cultivating positive relationships between all of the family members involved.

One stepmother put it beautifully as she described the effects of four *b'nei mitzvah* ceremonies on the children involved. "My biological children watch the videotape of their stepbrother's bar mitzvah with glee, but also with minds of detectives. Who is that relative? Tell me about him/her. My stepchildren have forged new relationships with my extended family. Collective memories are the mortar that will eventually cement our family into some type of configuration."[6]

BAR/BAT MITZVAH GUIDELINES

What follows are some suggested guidelines for divorced parents of a bar or bat mitzvah as they plan for the celebration.

1. Think about the welfare of your child and not about yourselves.

    You and your former spouse need to remember that this day is a major milestone in the life of your child. It should not be an occasion to make the child miserable as the two of you relive the past and find ways to get even with one another.

2. Take ample time to get ready.

    Usually the date of the bar or bat mitzvah is reserved on the temple calendar a minimum of one year in advance. There can be no excuses for not dealing with all contingencies and problems properly. A divorce may make it harder to do so and more tempting to either procrastinate or act impulsively. But proper planning becomes even more crucial for a divorced family than it was when the family was intact.

    Whomever the synagogue has designated to handle the arrangements will meet with both of you to review all of the specifics. If meeting together is too difficult, separate meetings can be arranged. If a family counselor or mediator would be helpful in getting over the rough spots, that also can be provided.

3. The synagogue is open to everyone.

    The synagogue is not a private club that a family reserves and then unilaterally decides whom to invite. That may be true for the reception, but not for the bar or bat mitzvah ceremony, which is an integral part of the worship service and is open to everyone. Efforts to stop a person from being present are simply unacceptable.

4. Rituals can be modified.

    The bar or bat mitzvah format can be adjusted as warranted by the circumstances. For example, if it is customary for the entire family to stand on the bimah and pass the Torah from one parent to the other and then to the celebrant, revisions can be made or another option introduced. Unless one parent has virtually abandoned the family or mistreated the child, both father and mother should have a role in what transpires. The nature of that role is open to discussion.

5. Cooperate in planning the reception.

    Having a joint, simple kiddush for the entire congregation after the service would be a nice gesture if both parents can tolerate it. Planning individual receptions for one's own circle of friends outside of the synagogue is also proper, provided that the child does not feel pressured by parents trying to outdo one another by the glitz of their respective parties.

The synagogue's responsibility is to see to it that all of these matters are thoroughly clarified well in advance of the event so that there are no misunderstandings. In the final analysis, what matters most is that parents behave with dignity and with sensitivity in keeping with the sanctity of the occasion and the best interests of their child.

RABBINIC COMMENTS AND SUGGESTIONS

Over the years, rabbis have confronted a good many of issues touched upon here. A sampling of their comments and suggestions is included.

"We have determined that children are not to be made to feel different because their parents are divorced. We focus on the reality that parents divorce each other, not their children. The major problem occurs when one parent attempts to exclude the other from participation. Comments such as "I am paying the temple,' or 'I drive every day,' or 'If he is on the *bimah,* I will be ill' are met with the goal of bringing both sides to a reasonable position. Neither parent will be allowed to exclude or embarrass the other."

"We are as flexible as we can be with *aliyot.* Parents are given the option of coming up together. Sometimes the father prefers to be alone. In some cases, the mother and father have had separate *aliyot."*

"I discourage the parent from ever asking the child directly, "What do you want?' This puts the child in a no-win guilt-provoking situation."

"There are usually problems with the social after the service. Once a father threatened to cancel the ceremony and to pull the child out of the service because there was a problem with the reception. I stood him up against the wall and said, 'I'm not going to let you make a fool out of yourself and humiliate your child. If you do this, you will regret it for the rest of your life. Go out and think it over and come back when you're not so agitated.' The man phoned me an hour later to thank me profusely for keeping him from making a great mistake."

The most hopeful comment was this one: "The bar/bat mitzvah process can be therapeutic for divorcing families. It can be a way to improve or reestablish communication—to put all problems in perspective and to bring those who have been estranged into at least a cordiality which can only benefit, since the child is not getting a divorce."[7]

There are some additional concerns rabbis may have to address in sorting through the complexities attendant to the bar/bat mitzvah event. One of these is to be fully prepared to raise any and all questions related to the divorce, which could affect the ceremony, if the parents fail to do so. Parents are not always forthcoming. They may be embarrassed or still too angry and upset to be totally open. The last thing the rabbi should want are surprises on bar or bat mitzvah day.

A related matter is to be careful not to rely upon only one parent's version of a situation. One rabbi phoned me asking for advice after the father of the bat mitzvah had told him that the girl's mother had no interest in being a part of the ceremony. I suggested that he contact the mother and find out what she wanted to do. As it turned out, contrary to the father's claims, the mother was indeed willing and eager to participate.

WHEN A SON OR DAUGHTER MARRIES

The marriage of a child will often awaken many of the same emotions stirred up by a bar or bat mitzvah. Memories that have been repressed and long-forgotten grudges may now surface once more. Hopefully, unless the divorce of the parents is recent, the passage of time will have enabled everyone to set aside the past and, at the very least, be civil to one another on this joyous occasion.

Unlike the comparative helplessness and fears of a thirteen-year-old child, the bride or groom should be quite outspoken regarding parental roles during the ceremony. A daughter can decide if she wants her father to escort her down the aisle. Who will pay for the wedding, who stands under the *chupah,* and who will be invited are other choices to be made. A parent may even be told, if the circumstances warrant, that he or she is not welcome.

All of these matters should be discussed with the rabbi who is officiating at the ceremony. If, for whatever reason, the couple fails to raise some of these questions, the rabbi should raise them tactfully. Like the bar or bat mitzvah, innovations in the ritual can easily be introduced in the interests of harmony and the well-being of all concerned.

WHEN PARENTS REMARRY

In the event of a second marriage following a divorce, parents may want their children to stand under the *chupah* with them. It can be a lovely moment. It is also one that can be marred if the former spouse takes this occasion to be negative and derogatory in an effort to poison the children's feelings about the new stepparent.

Individuals who act in this manner do so at their own risk. Their attitudes may well backfire and result in their children becoming alienated from them. It can also be a contributing factor regarding how well children adjust to new family structures created by their natural parents. Wherever possible, rabbis can again play an important role in helping the former spouse who is engaging in this kind of behavior to recognize its folly.

GRANDPARENTS HAVE RIGHTS TOO

Grandparents have always been the keepers of tradition and play a unique role in the lives of their grandchildren. Judaism teaches that the crown of elders is their grandchildren. In Deut. 4:9, we read that the people of Israel are to make God's teachings known to "your children and your children's children," a verse the rabbis explain as referring to the role of grandparents in the Jewish education of their grandchildren.

Since multigenerational families will be the rule rather than the exception in the years ahead, their importance in the family will only be enhanced. Already, a growing number of divorced mothers and even fathers either have moved back into their parents' homes or are relying upon them for financial support after a divorce.

The stereotype of all grandparents retiring to southern climes or isolating themselves in self-contained communities with only periodic contact with their grandchildren is a far less common phenomenon than it once might have been. Even when it is true, the advent of e-mail, faxes, and reduced travel rates for persons over sixty-five has facilitated ongoing communication between the generations.

After interviewing 700 grandparents and their grandchildren, researchers came to the following conclusions:

1. The grandparent-grandchild bond is second only in emotional importance to that between parents and children.

2. Problems that were passed on from grandparents to parents are not directly passed from grandparents to grandchildren.

3. Grandparents and grandchildren simply need one another.[8]

The love of grandparents for their grandchildren no more ceases because parents are divorcing than the love of parents for their children ends when the family unit unravels. Unfortunately, grandparents have become unwitting victims of ill will and custody battles between divorcing couples. Reports of efforts being made to deny them opportunities for visits with their grandchildren have increased.

Most states have made provision for grandparental visitation rights. Some also have laws allowing grandparents to file for full custody if parents have abandoned their children, are deemed unfit, or have died. But for grandparents to be forced to take legal action in order to see their grandchildren is a sorry state of affairs. In turn, they have the obligation to exercise great care and discretion when sons or daughters are divorcing.

The temptation to take sides and to be protective of one's own flesh and blood is certainly understandable. However, openly maligning the other parent in front of grandchildren is not acceptable and can only fuel that parent's hostility and harden his or her resolve to prevent the children from having any contact with the grandparents.

In an unforgettable mediation, a couple asked if both sets of grandparents could be present at a session. The couple themselves had parted on reasonably good terms and had determined that they would limit the disruption to their children's lives as much as possible. They encouraged continuing regular contact by the children with their grandparents.

The divorce had come as a terrible blow to the grandparents, who were inconsolable. Each side began accusing the other of undue interference in the couple's lives while they were married, thereby contributing by their actions to the breakup. As a result, whenever the grandchildren were in either home, the grandparents insisted upon making derogatory comments not only about the other parent but about the other grandparents as well.

It had reached a point where the grandchildren had become so upset and so unhappy that they no longer wished to visit. When told why their grandchildren would not visit them, the grandparents refused to listen. They accused the parents of poisoning the children against them. In the blindness caused by their terrible pain, they could not understand their own complicity in what had happened.

The divorcing couple had reached the end of their patience. Each had tried to reason with their respective mother and father, but to no avail. They pressed them to come to a mediation session. The grandparents agreed to do so only after it had been made perfectly clear that unless they did, they would have no opportunity, short of a court order, to see their grandchildren in the future.

It was the first time since the divorce that the entire family had been together in the same room. At first there was great tension. No one spoke. At last one of the grandfathers said, "You know, we haven't been together like this since the seder two years ago." Mention of the seder, which had been a family tradition for many years, broke the silence. Everyone began to talk at once. It was clear that both families still had great affection for one another but had not known what to do with their feelings after the divorce.

The families were now able to focus on the grandparents' behavior in a calm and reasoned way that was neither rejecting nor angry. The grandparents listened to what was being said and promised to try and stop looking for scapegoats. It was agreed that everyone would return for another session to talk some more. Some time with a family therapist was suggested. It was a successful end to what otherwise might have resulted in the permanent estrangement of these grandchildren from their grandparents.

On the other hand, the story of Dena and Ben was not as promising. They were a couple in their late seventies who had not seen their nine-year-old granddaughter in the year since their son had divorced his wife. During that time, she had moved to another community, which even in the best of circumstances would have made visits more difficult. The relationship with their daughter-in-law had never been a good one. Now she had decided to stop the child from having any contact with them.

In their grief, they had come to me for help. What they wanted was not legal advice, which they had already gotten and were reluctant to follow. They had no wish to cause their grandchild any further stress. They were searching for spiritual comfort. I shared my hope with them that at some point the mother would relent or that the child, as she grew older and more independent, would reach out to them on her own. It was not possible to know when, if ever, that would take place. In the meantime, they would have to bear the burden of this terrible loss and wait. They could still write letters to her and send gifts on her birthday and on Chanukah. There was always a chance that her mother would relent and allow her to receive them.

I suggested looking into the availability of a grandparents group where they could share their pain and anguish with others facing similar deprivations. Here again, synagogues and Jewish family agencies should consider establishing groups of this kind. Convincing grandparents to take part in a group of this nature may prove to be difficult, as those most in need of help may be reluctant to "go public" with their pain.

I also encouraged them to find solace in prayer and in the synagogue service. Perhaps, I said, as they shared words such as these with other worshipers, they would find some comfort:

> Each of us enters this sanctuary with a different need.
>
> Some hearts are full of gratitude and joy: They are overflowing with the happiness of love and the joy of life; they are eager to confront the day, to make the world more fair; they are recovering from illness or have escaped misfortune. And we rejoice with them.
>
> Some hearts ache with sorrow: Disappointments weigh heavily upon them, and they have tasted despair; families have been broken; loved ones lie on a bed of pain; death has taken those whom they cherished. May our presence and sympathy bring them comfort.
>
> Some hearts are embittered: They have sought answers in vain; ideals are mocked and betrayed; life has lost its meaning and value. May the knowledge that we too are searching, restore their hope and give them courage to believe that not all is emptiness.
>
> Some spirits hunger: They long for friendship; they crave understanding; they yearn for warmth. May we in our common need and striving gain strength from one another, as we share our joys, lighten each other's burdens, and pray for the welfare of our community.[9]

FAMILIES MAY LOOK DIFFERENT TODAY, BUT THE ISSUES HAVEN'T CHANGED

More and more Jewish men and women are entering into relationships that do not adhere to the traditional model of the nuclear family. When conflicts take place or the relationships come to an end, struggles similar to those facing married couples who divorce occur. The needs of these men and women for acceptance and support by the Jewish community are no less acute than they are when conventional relationships come apart.

CONFLICTS OVER PATERNITY

In many states, once a claim of paternity is validated, a child's father may be entitled to the same rights of parenting and visitation as those accorded a divorced father. He is also subject to the same child support obligations.

Frank, who was Jewish, and Elsa, who was Catholic, had come to mediation during her final month of pregnancy. Not only was the couple not married, their dislike of one another was so palpable that it led one to wonder how and why they had been attracted to each other in the first place.

Amniocentesis had revealed that the baby would be a boy. Frank was demanding that the child be ritually circumcised and raised as a Jew. Elsa was just as adamant that neither would take place. If he persisted, she threatened to have the baby baptized and raised as a Catholic. At the first mediation session, Frank accused Elsa of "setting him up" and of never having any interest in him other than as a sperm donor, a charge that she vehemently denied.

Whatever its accuracy, their relationship, however fleeting, was now destined to become a mutually antagonistic, lifetime association. After endless wrangling, it was agreed that the baby would be circumcised, but without any formal Jewish ceremony. There would also be no baptism. The question of the child's religious identity would be postponed until some later date after other aspects of parenting responsibilities had been clarified, such as child support and visitation by Frank.

Barring some miraculous change of attitude by both individuals, it was clear that years of constant tension and conflict between them, which would inevitably affect this as yet unborn infant, were in the offing. All that could be

54

done at this moment to counter that probability had taken place. The rest would have to be dealt with as it occurred.

A second case involved Rose and Henry, both of whom were Jewish. Rose had been married briefly after finishing high school. That marriage had ended in divorce, and she had been single for nearly twenty years. Henry, recently divorced, with three children of his own, was still married when he met Rose at a party. They were attracted to each other, and Rose had asked Henry if he would consider fathering a child with her. Her biological clock was running out, she had said, and she had no prospects for marriage.

The one condition she imposed was that upon conception, Henry agree to waive all claims to paternity and promise never to see her or the baby again. Henry concurred, although no written agreement was ever signed. Rose was artificially inseminated using Henry's sperm. She gave birth to a boy and, in keeping with their understanding, did not inform him of the birth.

Some years later, Henry suddenly appeared, informing Rose that he had divorced his wife, and although he did not wish to marry her, he did want to claim his paternal rights regarding the boy. He was fully prepared, he said, to pay child support and do whatever else was required in return for a visitation schedule that he considered to be fair. To complicate matters further, the child, now seven, had been told that his father had died and consequently had no inkling of Henry's existence.

After much negotiation, Rose reluctantly agreed to a period of trial visitation. In return, Henry, with equal ambivalence, consented to a full psychological evaluation of himself, the child, and Rose, which would become part of the record when a final determination was made regarding the nature and amount of visitation he would be granted. Couples' therapy was also agreed to by both of them.

The full import of this turn of events would take years to assess, not to speak of the as yet unknown effects the sudden appearance of Henry would have upon a child who had believed his father to be dead.

The situations described here are no longer uncommon. They are symptomatic of the wide range of diverse family households now composing the American Jewish community, which will only increase in the years ahead. Recognizing this state of affairs, any number of Reform congregations have revised their bylaws defining membership so as to allow for a much broader definition of what constitutes a household for purposes of synagogue affiliation.

GAY AND LESBIAN RELATIONSHIPS

While paternity is one issue, a more significant development is the challenge posed to the synagogue by the needs of gay and lesbian members, both as individuals and as families. Orthodox and Conservative Judaism have remained adamant in their rejection of homosexuality as an acceptable sexual orientation. Both movements have called upon gays and lesbians either to live outwardly as heterosexuals or, if this is not possible, to remain celibate. These are the criteria for their acceptance as identified Orthodox or Conservative Jews.

Reform Judaism has been far more open and supportive. It has ordained gay and lesbian rabbis and welcomed gay and lesbian congregations as members of the UAHC. As previously mentioned, a growing number of Reform congregations have revised their bylaws to make the definition of family membership much more inclusive than ever before. Specific references to gay and lesbian relationships have been emphasized, and these men and women have been encouraged to become members of the congregation.

The CCAR has gone on record calling for the approval of the right to civil marriage in all fifty states for homosexuals, for their entitlement to medical insurance and other benefits granted to heterosexual married couples, and for the passage of legislation protecting them against violence and discrimination. After much deliberation over whether Reform rabbis should officiate at same-sex ceremonies, that determination was left to the discretion of every rabbi.

As gays and lesbians enter into domestic partnerships and adopt or arrange to have children by means of any of the alternative reproductive technologies now available, conflicts are as predictable as they are with heterosexual couples. The story of Helene and Arnold is a poignant example.

Helene, a lesbian, had asked a gay friend named Arnold if he would agree to be a sperm donor so that she might have a child. Arnold agreed, promising as well in deference to Helen's wishes that he would not seek any parental privileges. Again, nothing was put in writing. When the baby was born, Arnold changed his mind.

A bitter court battle ensued, with the court ruling in Arnold's favor, granting him visitation rights and obligating him to pay child support. For Helene, the ruling of the court was incomprehensible. In turn, Arnold was devastated by what he felt was Helene's cruelty in opposing his right to visit the child. The animosity between them was so intense that in frustration, their attorneys asked that mediation be tried in hopes that it might succeed where litigation had failed. With much reservation, we agreed to mediate.

The parties came to try and work out a mutually acceptable parenting schedule. It was a very tense scene. Helene had never forgiven Arnold for demanding parenting rights, and he remained livid at her forcing a court battle over what he felt were his basic prerogatives as a father.

It was evident that the child's best interests were being completely neglected in the heat of their rage at one another. All efforts to point this out were futile. Finally it became necessary to terminate the mediation, which was now serving primarily as a vehicle for both sides to continue their diatribes against one another.

The two of them returned to the courts seeking the satisfaction they would never find, given their relentless hostility and their desire for vengeance. Sadly, in this setting, the child whom they both professed to love, and undoubtedly did, was destined to pay a terrible psychological price in the years ahead.

It is hard to assess what influence a rabbi might have brought to bear in helping these individuals deal differently with the situation just described. But incidents such as these are illustrative of some of the new conditions of Jewish family life that will inevitably confront the synagogue and other community institutions in the twenty-first century.

ABUSE IN THE JEWISH FAMILY

An open secret of contemporary Jewish life is the incidence of spousal and child abuse in Jewish families. Only in recent years has the prevailing myth that Jews do not engage in these acts been shattered. At long last, synagogues and Jewish family agencies not only have spoken forcefully against such behavior, but have conducted educational programs regarding them as well. Both the Conservative and Reform movements have published books and other materials on the subject.[10] Orthodox women's groups have opened shelters for abused women in this country and in Israel. The incidence of abuse in Israel is particularly disturbing.

It is estimated that more than 200,000 women in the Jewish state suffer from some form of domestic abuse. There are almost daily reports in Israeli newspapers regarding such incidents as a rabbi hitting and kicking his wife before going off to services and then resuming upon his return, a policeman beating his wife because she failed to light Shabbat candles, and a man who upon returning from military reserve duty awakens his wife in the middle of the night and threatens to kill her if she does not tell him with whom she has been cheating on him. The problem becomes even worse in the aftermath of Jewish holidays, which seem to exacerbate such behavior.[11]

In the past, the victims were either ignored or made to feel as if somehow they deserved what had happened to them. Women, in particular, had nowhere to turn and were forced to resign themselves to their fates, having no recourse but to bear their suffering and their humiliation silently.

When dealing with wife battering, Jewish tradition presents a rather mixed picture. Some rabbinic authorities not only were disinclined to permit a get, they sanctioned wife beating if it could be shown that the wife had provoked her husband by her actions.

No less a personality than Maimonides maintained that beating a bad wife was an acceptable form of discipline. A later sage, Moses Isserles, distinguished between wife beating done capriciously and that done out of necessity.[12] The observation of the thirteenth-century rabbinic authority Meir of Rothenburg that "Jews are not addicted to the prevalent habit of beating their wives" conveys a rather ambigious impression regarding the extent of this practice among Jews.[13]

That it may have been all too frequent is more directly attested to by another rabbinic authority, Simchah ben Shmuel, who writes, "A man who does this should be put under a ban and excommunicated and flogged.... If he wants to divorce her, let him do so and give her the *ketubah* payment."[14]

In our own day, allegations of spousal abuse are not only all too common, they are often raised in the course of a bitter divorce proceeding and need to be carefully investigated before arriving at any conclusions.

When Lotte and George came to their first mediation session, they were extremely nervous. Lotte said "I wonder if I should be in an attorney's office rather than here." She then related that the night before George had moved out of the house, they had a terrible quarrel. In a momentary rage, George had pushed her to the floor. She, in turn, had thrown a plate at his head.

They both agreed that it had been the first and only time this had happened in over nine years of marriage and many arguments. They were embarrassed and equally contrite. Under the circumstances, it was our considered opinion, that this was not a true example of spousal abuse and would not interfere with the mediation. Our intuition proved to be accurate.

RAPE

Whatever the historic rabbinic ambiguities regarding wife beating, marital rape was another matter entirely. The Talmud states that a man is forbidden to compel his wife to the mitzvah of *onah* (intercourse).Rabbi Joshua ben Levi adds, "Whosoever compels his wife to the 'mitzvah' will have unworthy children" (B. *Eruvin* l00b).

Conjugal relations were also not permitted if a man was angry at his wife, was drunk, had decided to divorce her, or was thinking about another woman while engaging in lovemaking. (B. *N'darim* 28b). The Rabbis speak of *simchat ishto,* literally meaning the gratification of one's wife. It was a man's duty to see to her sexual needs, but not under the demeaning conditions just mentioned.

Accounts of husbands' assuming that they are free to force themselves on their wives as a marital prerogative are all too familiar. The story of Max and Louise is a prime example. Max was a heavy drinker who despite his wife's pleadings had refused to get any help for his addiction. Louise tearfully reported that while drunk he had raped her. Max, unrepentant, blamed what had happened on overdrinking. "Besides," he said, "she is my wife."

When I pointed out that according to the rabbis, the definition of *derech eretz* included the admonition that a bridegroom not enter the bridal chamber until invited to do so by the bride, he smiled and said derisively, "How quaint." When informed of the passage in the Talmud that unequivocally forbade the rape of one's wife, he was unmoved.

It was clear that mediation would not be helpful in this situation. Louise would need the support of a strong advocate in the days ahead. Max would require the intervention of a good therapist as well.

SEXUAL ABUSE OF CHILDREN

Judaism is explicit in its condemnation of the sexual abuse of children. The passages from chapter 18 of Leviticus that are read in the synagogue on the Day of Atonement condemn incest in the most powerful of terms. Leviticus 18:6, which is then expanded in subsequent verses, states: "None of you shall come near anyone of his own flesh to uncover nakedness, I am the Lord."

Allegations about fathers molesting their children, especially when they are in their care after a divorce, have skyrocketed in recent years. A number of these cases have been dramatized on television, and others have made national headlines. Episodes of mothers refusing to abide by court-ordered visits of children to their fathers or a court's award of custody to the father because of their belief that the child has been sexually molested are no longer rare. Some mothers have kidnapped their children and gone into hiding with them rather than comply. A few have actually gone to jail for violating a judge's ruling.

Jewish parents and even grandparents are not immune from this type of behavior. A charge of child abuse needs to be taken seriously. At the same time, a suspicious parent should use good judgment before taking any formal action. Before the parent jumps to conclusions, it may be advisable to contact the alleged abuser and tell him or her about the child's complaints and what actions are being contemplated should they prove to be true. There may be times when the whole matter is a misunderstanding that can be clarified by discussion with one's former spouse.

A child's behavior may be erratic and unpredictable after a divorce. Insomnia, bed-wetting, irritability, not wanting to go on visits, and once there, not wanting to go home are all familiar patterns. What a child says has to be evaluated carefully.

In a case reported in mediation, a six-year-old girl named Sheri told her mother that Daddy was lying down with her in bed at night. "Daddy touched me all over," she added. Instead of panicking, the mother called the father, told him what the child had said, and demanded an explanation.

The father acknowledged that because Sheri was anxious and fussy in her new room in the apartment to which he had moved, he had begun lying down with her at bedtime, as he had done when the family was intact. In trying to get her to go to sleep, he had rubbed her back, an act that the child had described as "touching all over."

The parents agreed to meet with the child's pediatrician and get some guidance regarding how to respond to the child's anxiety over the divorce. The doctor also met with Sheri to talk about the "touching." Because the parents were cooperative, they acted sensibly. The situation did not get out of hand and did not end up in court.

In a second case, eight-year-old Donna had told her mother that Daddy kissed her on the lips and it was "yucky." The mother immediately phoned the father, who explained that what happened was that Donna had actually kissed him in acting out a scene she had witnessed on TV. The mother, relieved, ignored the incident.

A week later, however, when the child complained that "Daddy pinched me down there" and pointed to her genitals, she took her to the hospital for an examination. The evaluating team determined that what the child had described had indeed occurred. A formal investigation followed.

Certainly all charges about child abuse need to be taken seriously. At the same time, using good judgment is essential. The only thing conceivably worse than an actual act of abuse by a parent is a false accusation that it has taken place. The prospect of one parent bearing false witness against the other, no matter how bad the marriage and angry the divorce, is horrendous and should never occur. The spectacle of parents lying about each other's behavior can only further damage a child's emotional well-being.

5

RESOLVING
QUESTIONS OF
ALIMONY:

THE LEGACY OF THE *KETUBAH*

There is a poignant statement in the Jerusalem Talmud that says that if a man's former wife falls into need, he should remember that once she had been his flesh, and therefore he "must stretch out his hand and succor her" (J. *K'tubot* 34b). Another midrashic tale relates the generosity of Rabbi Jose, who, upon hearing that his former wife and her second husband had fallen on hard times let them live in a house that he owned and provided for them for the rest of their lives (*Leviticus Rabbah* 34:14).

But these were nonlegal statements that had no authority other than a moral one. They were not technically enforceable in a Jewish court of law. The *ketubah,* on the other hand, which was signed by the bride and groom before a marriage, was the most important legal document a woman possessed. Not only did it prevent her husband from divorcing her at will, it deprived him of any claim to her assets after a divorce.

Furthermore, it gave her assurances of what we know as alimony, to be paid out of her husband's personal assets, and implied additional benefits, which, although not specified in the *ketubah,* were imposed by the *beit din.* These included the following:

1. Her redemption by her husband from captivity.

2. Medical care, should she become ill.

3. Should she predecease her husband, her sons and not his from another marriage would inherit (1) the *ketubah,* (2) a sum of money her husband had to pay, and (3) return of her dowry.

4. If she outlived her husband, her daughters could continue to live in the home and be supported from his estate until they married.

5. She could remain in the family home after her husband's death and maintain herself from his estate as long as she stayed there.

Once divorced, a woman's economic well-being could be very tenuous, especially if she were older and her prospects for remarriage were slim. Generally, if she did not remarry and, for whatever the reasons, the provisions of the *ketubah* did not apply or the funds left by her husband were negligible, she was forced to live with relatives or, in some instances in medieval Jewish communities, to find work as a servant in the homes of the well-to-do.

For these reasons, the *ketubah* served as a major impediment to a husband's arbitrary behavior and possible ill-treatment of her. A wife's possession of her *ketubah* was so important that Jewish law required her to keep it with her at all times. Should it be lost or misplaced, the couple could not continue to live together until another one was written.

Although there are some parallels between the intent of the *ketubah* and the modern concept of alimony as a form of financial insurance for a woman after a divorce, they stem from utterly different worlds. The term *alimony* is derived from the Latin word for nourishment. In the past, it was customary for divorced women to receive alimony for as long as a lifetime, depending upon the length of the marriage. Payment would cease only if they were to remarry.

Lifetime alimony was predicated on the assumption that women were destined to be homemakers with few independent assets and little or no potential for gainful employment in a male-dominated culture. Most women had never worked outside of the home, having literally gone from their status as daughter to that of wife and mother.

The concept was derived from the practice of English ecclesiastical courts in the eighteenth century to allow married couples to live apart without divorce. When this occurred, the husband was responsible for the wife's economic well-being, since by law all of her assets had reverted to him when they married.

Today the criteria for the payment of alimony are far different than they once were. A woman's age, the number of minor children at home, her educational and professional training, her employment status, and the length of her marriage are all factors that will be considered in deciding the amount of alimony and the length of time it will be paid. Alimony may be designated as temporary or rehabilitative. It can be restricted to the completion of a requisite course of study in a particular field.

On occasion, no alimony may be awarded, if it can be demonstrated to the court's satisfaction that the woman is already gainfully employed, she is independently wealthy, or her professional credentials assure her a steady income and there are no dependent children at home. There may even be times when a woman's assets are greater than those of her husband's and she will be required to pay him alimony.

These are complicated issues that require not only the expertise of professionals but the goodwill and cooperation of the divorcing parties as well.

However reluctant some men may be to pay child support, their willingness to pay alimony is often equally problematic, but it usually fails to attract the same notoriety attached to the delinquency of so-called deadbeat dads.

It is here that the biblical verse found in Gen. 2:18, which speaks of Eve as Adam's helpmate, *ezer k'negdo,* takes on special meaning. Judaism's portrayal of men as incomplete, as not fully formed without a woman's companionship, is most instructive. The rabbis go even further when they refer to a man's wife as his *bayit,* the Hebrew word for home, in stressing the unique contribution a wife makes to a marriage.

Men need to be mindful of the many years during a marriage when their wives deferred or even suspended the pursuit of their own career and ambitions in order to support their husband and raise a family. They tend to forget that no computer or calculator can measure the true value of a marriage and what each partner has actually contributed to it. These are intangibles that are not quantifiable in dollars and cents, since without them, no relationship can flourish.

A case in point is the story of Sam and Eva. They had come to mediate their divorce and had specifically wanted to do so with a rabbi, since they were observant Jews and synagogue members. Sam, who had an excellent Jewish background, took particular pleasure in quoting biblical and rabbinic passages whenever the opportunity presented itself.

The couple had been childhood sweethearts. Unfortunately, they had grown apart over the years. Divorce had been reluctantly decided upon only after much soul searching and genuine efforts at resolving their differences, all to no avail.

The mediation had proceeded smoothly. The one angry encounter occurred in the course of determining how long Sam would be expected to support Eva financially in order for her to complete her professional training, pay off some substantial school loans, and start her own career. The issue was not a matter of affordability, since Sam was quite comfortable.

"How long is this going to go on?" he shouted. "Haven't I done enough already?" Eva was just as vehement as she spoke of what she had sacrificed and delayed in his behalf, how she now found herself at the age of forty-one having to finish a program she should have completed twenty years earlier. "How do you put a price on that?" she cried.

The impasse was broken when I reminded Sam of the verse in Genesis referring to Eve as Adam's helpmate and pointed out all that Eva had done during their years together. I then cited the passage from Song of Songs 1:16, "They put me in charge of the vineyards, but I neglected my own." The time had come, I added, for Eva to cultivate her own vineyard. It struck a cord. Sam nodded, and Eva began to weep. It was a moving, even beautiful moment, the divorce notwithstanding. A settlement that both Sam and Eva could accept was reached.

In the case of Betsy and David, the citation of biblical verses would not be of much use. They had come to mediation reluctantly, at the urging of friends whose judgment they respected. Their anger at one another was so intense that as mediators we had our doubts regarding their ability to mediate, doubts we openly expressed.

Nevertheless, all agreed to try and see how things went. The couple had been married for eighteen years and had four children, aged nine to fourteen. The marriage had always been plagued by conflict. Betsy had asked for a divorce shortly after the bar mitzvah of their son. David had refused to consider it. In desperation, Betsy told him that for the past two years she had been involved with another man, a relationship, she came to understand in therapy, that had been a way of forcing the issue. "I kept trying to tell you," she said, "but you just wouldn't listen."

The sticking point in the mediation was the payment of alimony, which David found inconceivable in light of the affair. He recognized that given the length of their marriage and Betsy's need to complete her training as a registered nurse, he was legally required to pay alimony. But her admission of adultery, whatever the reasons for it, had devastated him.

He would repeat over and over the number of times during their marriage when he, despite his own unhappiness and frustrations, had rejected sexual overtures from other women because he was a married man. Now, he said, to give Betsy alimony would reward her for her infidelity.

Betsy admitted she had made a mistake and voiced her regret for hurting him so deeply. It was, she said, the only way she could make him see that their relationship was over. Whatever time-limited financial support he gave her would enable both of them to get on with their lives and undo the error they had made together, eighteen years earlier.

In her heart, Betsy had not intended to be David's helpmate. She knew that she had never provided the companionship he had wanted in a wife. "David," she pleaded, "you deserve someone who can give you what you need. I know I haven't done so. I regret it not only for your sake, but for mine and the children's as well. These payments will help us both start over. I would like us to part as friends, however strange that may sound."

The payment of alimony was part of recognizing that they had spent eighteen years together and had parented four children. Despite it all, when they thought about it, they could point to joyful and fulfilling moments together as a couple and as a family. Whatever else had gone on between them, these moments could not be ignored. Unfortunately, there had been too few of them, and there was no chance for a reconciliation.

Some months later, I bumped into David on the street. He told me that since the divorce, he had met a woman and really felt good about the new relationship, although as he put it, "I'm still a little gun-shy." He felt much more comfortable about the alimony, and while the hurt was still there, he understood more about Betsy's behavior, even though he still was unable to condone it. They saw each other periodically and maintained as much contact as was necessary for the sake of the children, who were doing reasonably well.

He wondered if I could suggest a meditation or prayer for a new relationship. He wasn't sure where it was going to go or what his capacity for trust really was after everything that had happened, but he was determined to try. Somehow, seeing me, he added, had reawakened the idea of praying at a time like this. He wasn't sure that he would ever recite the prayers but wanted them anyway. I promised to look into the matter and wished him well.

David's request for a prayer to recite as he undertook this relationship was a very positive step in coming to terms with the past and building a new life for himself.

MEDITATIONS UPON STARTING
A NEW RELATIONSHIP

God, at this moment I acknowledge my anxiety and my elation. I rejoice in the potential of a new friend's caring and affection, and yet I confess my fears as well. Grant me the courage to reach out to another and the strength to bear disappointment should my hopes not come to pass. Allow me to trust in new beginnings and to go forth with open arms and a willing heart. Blesssed are You O God, whose name is goodness, and to whom it is pleasant to give thanks. (Anonymous)

There are times when each of us feels lost or alone, adrift and forsaken, unable to reach those next to us, or to be reached by them. And there are days and nights when existence seems to lack all purpose, and our lives seem brief sparks in an indifferent cosmos.

Fear and loneliness enter into the soul. None of us is immune from doubt and fear; none escapes times when all seems dark and senseless. Then, at the ebb-tide of the spirit, the soul cries out and reaches for companionship.[1]

> As the moon sinks on the mountain-edge
> The fisherman's lights flicker.
> Far out on the dark wide sea.

> When we think that we are alone
> Are steering our ships at midnight,
> We hear the splash of oars
> Far beyond us.[2]

6

WHEN INTERMARRIED COUPLES DIVORCE:

PROMISES ABOUT RAISING CHILDREN AS JEWS

Since the end of World War II, interfaith marriage in the United States has burgeoned. It is currently estimated that one out of every two marriages involving a born Jew is an intermarriage and that some 700,000 children now live in homes where one parent is not Jewish.[1] As we enter the twenty-first century, there is every indication that this pattern will continue unabated.

In the past, it has been theorized that intermarriage was a way for alienated Jews to deny their identities and become part of the majority culture. When it came to rearing children, more often than not they were raised as Christian or, at the very least, with no religious orientation. By and large, they and their families were ultimately lost to the Jewish community.

Current studies reveal that the conversion rate to Judaism has declined, and a large number of couples in interfaith marriages are not raising their children as Jews.[2] Even so, quite a few couples in marriages where one partner has retained his or her non-Jewish identity are identified with the Jewish community. They are joining synagogues and are enrolling their children in religious schools.

But there is also a downside to this phenomenon. When intermarried couples divorce, and at least statistically they do so at a higher rate than couples of the same faith, a growing source of contention has been the nature of their children's religious upbringing now that the marriage is over.[3] It is feared that this struggle will become even more common in the years ahead.

Cases in which premarital promises stipulating that a child will be raised as a Jew that have now allegedly been broken are being brought before civil courts. In each instance, the plaintiff has been the Jewish father and the defendant the child's mother. In general, the mother had not converted to Judaism. Where she did, she renounced her Jewish identity at the time of the divorce or shortly thereafter and reverted back to her original faith.

Fathers are complaining that before the marriage, these women had promised verbally that their children would be raised as Jews. These promises, they insist, are binding and should be as enforceable as any other legal contract. Ironically, the precedent for claiming that verbal promises about the religious upbringing of children of intermarried couples are contractually binding was set in a custody battle involving two Orthodox Jewish parents, Sharon and Elliott Friederwitzer. The issue here had nothing whatsoever to do with conversion or intermarriage.

The Friederwitzers were divorced in the state of New York in 1979. Mrs. Friederwitzer had agreed to rear their children as Orthodox Jews as part of the divorce agreement. The father sued for custody on the grounds that his former wife had violated the agreement, because the children no longer attended Sabbath services regularly and because the mother's new boyfriend turned on the TV set on both Friday evening and Saturday morning.

In ruling in the father's favor, the court said: "Such contradictions can only cause confusion in the minds of children of tender years and be detrimental to the development of religious feelings."[4]

The issue has been complicated even further by revisions in the divorce laws of all fifty states granting both parents the opportunity, already mentioned, to have some form of shared legal custody of their children after a divorce.

Formerly, the religious, educational, and medical needs of a child were left solely to the judgment of the custodial parent. The other parent could suggest, but his or her preferences were of no consequence in deciding the matter. The introduction of shared legal custody, it was felt, would give the noncustodial parent a greater sense of participation in the life of a child after a divorce and thereby benefit both parent and child. But as with other divorce reforms, the resulting religious complications were not foreseen.

An entire body of legal literature has developed dealing with the constitutionality of a court's role in deciding what in the past were considered to be sectarian religious disputes. One leading divorce attorney put it most succinctly: "This is going to be the up and coming area of family law. It touches on every aspect of the 1st Amendment, freedom of religion, freedom of speech, freedom of association."[5]

Those opposed to a civil court's intervention in these matters have complained that in effect judges are now advancing or inhibiting religious expression by their rulings. One critic has written, "Judicial judgements of what constitutes a child's best interests have become a product of the personality, temperament, background, interests and biases of the trial judge or of the community that elected him."[6]

By way of illustration, in a case with which the author is personally familiar, a woman who had converted to Judaism premaritally at the behest of her husband-to-be chose to revert back to her former faith after their divorce. As the primary custodial parent, she continued to rear their son as a Jew, celebrating all Jewish holidays and seeing to it that the boy attended religious school regularly.

Her husband, however, took her to court and threatened to sue for custody, charging that although the child was being raised Jewishly, the mother observed Christmas, had a Christmas tree, and read stories about the baby Jesus to the little boy. These acts, he argued, were detrimental to the child's Jewish upbringing. He asked the court to order her to stop and, if she refused, to award him full custody of the boy.

The judge ruled in the mother's favor, saying that there was no indication that either the stories about Jesus or the celebration of Christmas were in any way harmful to the child's welfare or to his Jewish identity. Moreover, he continued, to rule otherwise would be to deprive the mother of her civil rights and her right to privacy in her own home.

The very fact that in this case one court ruled in favor of the mother, while in the Freiderwitzer case a separate court supported the father's contentions illustrates the utter unpredictability of the courts in settling disputes of this kind. No case can serve as a reliable precedent for any other.

Even when there is written documentation confirming a commitment to rear children as Jews, it may not be enough to sway a court of law. *In re marriage of Weiss,* a case brought before the California Appellate Court in 1998, is illustrative of this fact. Prior to the marriage of the couple involved, the woman, a Baptist, converted to Judaism.

At that time, she signed a "Declaration of Faith," witnessed by three rabbis, in which she pledged to raise all of the couple's children "in loyalty to the Jewish faith and its practices." They had one son. After their divorce, the husband went to court contending that his son was now being indoctrinated in the Christian faith and attended church summer camp. His wife said that this was true.

The trial court awarded joint physical and legal custody to both parents, allotted religious holidays to each parent, and authorized the child's enrollment in a Hebrew studies program. In addition, the trial court stated that nothing in its order was deemed to prevent either party from enrolling the child in or having the child participate in other religious programs or activities. The court of appeals upheld the ruling of the trial court.[7]

The inconsistent nature of court rulings in these matters makes the courts a less than desirable venue for their resolution, not to speak of the legal costs entailed in this process. Funds that could be used for education and the other needs of children are now being spent in bitter struggles over religious ideology.

To paraphrase an old adage, courts are indeed places of last resort. They were never intended to provide happy or even necessarily satisfying answers to controversies. Persons who believe that they can are deluding themselves. But there is an even more basic reason for avoiding the court system in resolving the question of a child's religious identity after divorce.

To think that a court can really settle a matter of this nature is misguided at best. While court orders can be quite effective in enforcing financial agreements and disposing of contested, tangible assets after divorce, the realm of religious belief is a very different matter.

Regulating what someone should or may not think is next to impossible. Doing so is even more problematic when children are involved. Furthermore, making children's religious beliefs a battlefield, even with the best of intentions, can only damage and disillusion those on whose behalf parents claim to be waging their struggle in the first place.

Imagine what children must experience, knowing that parents are in court arguing over what they will be allowed to think or celebrate. Picture their bewilderment as they are shuttled on varying days of the week to houses of worship and to religious schools that preach and teach differing, often contradictory messages.

Solving the problem of the religious upbringing of a child after the divorce of an intermarried couple remains among the most vexing and complex dilemmas confronting both the legal system and the synagogue in the next century. Thus far, attempted solutions have been less than satisfactory.

Ideally, in the best of all possible worlds, Jews and non-Jews who fall in love and decide to marry would hesitate before making hasty commitments about the religious upbringing of their as yet unborn children.

The desire to please a partner, the fantasy that love will conquer all, a sense that religion may not be that important, the conviction that somehow things can be worked out later and that now is not the time to rock the boat—all are factors that interfere with making sound judgments. Generally, one or more of these sentiments will dictate what the partner who is not Jewish will say when asked by their Jewish mate to agree to raise their children as Jews.

Furthermore, people and circumstances change during a marriage. What appeared to be a plausible decision during courtship may no longer be experienced in the same way at a later date, particularly when the marriage is coming apart. Divorce often serves as the impetus for a reevaluation of numerous life choices, including religious ones.

But if a courtroom is not the place for settling this issue, what should be done? One suggestion has been that couples write prenuptial agreements specifying what a child's religious upbringing is to be should the Jewish parent die or the couple divorce. A model prepared a number of years ago contained the following stipulations:

> The parties to this agreement...agree that religious training and practice are an important and integral part of our lives and our children's lives. It is our joint resolve that our children... receive a formal education in the Jewish religion.... Subsequent to their Bar or Bat Mitzvah our children should be provided with the opportunity to choose whether to continue their formal religious education.... Should one or both children reside in the care and custody of a single parent, we agree that parent shall carry out this provision to the best of his or her ability and shall cooperate with the noncustodial spouse to that end.[8]

Although prenuptial agreements have become more common with the increase in the number of second marriages, they have usually focused upon the disposition of a couple's assets after death or divorce. Few intermarried couples have been inclined to draft them with the question of a child's religious upbringing in mind.

Furthermore, it is unclear whether a court would recognize a clause of this nature as binding. The California Appellate Court did not, in its ruling in the Weiss case discussed above. One critic has noted, "Courts subject stipulations regarding children to a higher degree of scrutiny than they would apply to purely monetary disposition. In view of judicial hostility toward prior arrangements regarding custody and support, they should be avoided in the agreement."[9]

At one time, the Reform movement gave serious consideration to suggesting that intermarried couples draft prenuptial agreements. The idea was discarded not only because of the ambiguity over their enforcement in the courts, but because of what was deemed to be the awkward position of talking to a couple about divorce contingencies before their marriage.

The understandable reluctance to talk about divorce in a premarital setting may have to be reevaluated given the current climate of marital breakdown.

This is especially true in working with couples contemplating an interfaith marriage, where the question of a child's religious upbringing is so crucial.

Both Reform and Conservative Judaism conduct introduction to Judaism courses throughout the United States and Canada, intended for non-Jewish men and women wanting to learn more about Judaism. The majority of those enrolled in these classes are romantically involved with a Jewish partner. Some of them will convert to Judaism; others will not. Regardless of that decision, the likelihood is that these couples will marry and many will have children. It may be time, therefore, to consider the inclusion of some discussion about divorce and a child's Jewish identity as part of the curriculum.

When counseling couples who are intermarrying, rabbis also need to reassess the disinclination to talk about the problems of divorce and children. They might well raise the option of a prenuptial agreement, along with pointing out its shortcomings and the possible legal obstacles it could encounter. But given the growing number of courtroom confrontations of the kind described in this chapter, it is time for the Reform movement, which led the way in welcoming and integrating interfaith couples into the synagogue, to address this problem as well.

Perhaps thought should be given to the reestablishment of a modern version of the Jewish Conciliation Courts in New York City, which were utilized so effectively in the early years of this century to resolve conflicts between Jewish immigrants to these shores and avoid litigious proceedings in the secular court system. It is a novel, perhaps even impractical idea, but it still merits some serious consideration.

There are other courses of action for couples to consider in an effort to avoid the legal entanglements of courts and attorneys. Meeting with the rabbi who counseled them before their marriage and who may have officiated at their wedding is one. Much will depend upon how comfortable both partners feel with the rabbi, given the circumstances. If the couple or the rabbi has left the community in the intervening years, conferring with another rabbi whose specialty is working with intermarried couples also should be explored. Again, the availability of individuals with these credentials needs to be publicized so that people know where to turn.

Working with a family mediator who will assist the couple in drafting a set of guidelines that are in the best interests of their children is another possibility. Before doing either, there is a prior task, which may be the most difficult of all to accomplish, but without which couples will inevitably find themselves back in a courtroom. That is to try, however hard it may be, to think back and recall their feelings when conversations about children were first initiated.

Fathers might ask themselves: Did I threaten not to go through with the marriage unless "she" either formally converted to Judaism or at the very least agreed to raise our kids as Jews? Why didn't I realize that not only was it unfair to make a demand of that kind, but that pressure of this sort was potentially counterproductive and might come back to haunt me some day? Now that it has, what can I do to make it easier on everyone, especially our kids?

Mothers might ponder: How ambivalent was I when he asked me to do this and I said yes? Why did I go along if my reservations were there from the very beginning? Did I do so just to please him and his family? Have I been resentful all these years? Why didn't I say something until now? I am not an innocent victim. Given the past, he is not being totally unreasonable in his expectations. How can I meet him halfway? I don't want the children to suffer any more than they already have.

Setting aside this time for self-reflection may help both parties determine what are the true motives behind their present behavior. Are they based upon deep-seated convictions, or are they a way of getting even for a host of spoken and unspoken accumulated grievances, some of which may have nothing to do with the religious upbringing of their children?

In the author's experience, in more than a few of these cases, once the marriage took place, the parties involved were either nonobservant or tended to celebrate both Jewish and Christian holidays. Neither parent objected to these practices and sometimes encouraged them. Whatever the nature of their grievances over the years, religion was not one of them. It was only after divorce that the matter came to a head.

There were instances when the Jewish father who had been so insistent that his non-Jewish fiancee make religious concessions essentially abdicated his role in the religious life of the household after the marriage and relegated all responsibility for the Jewish upbringing of their child to his wife.

One very angry mother complained bitterly to me, "All he [her husband] cared about was my conversion so that he could keep his parents and his friends happy." Fortunately, in this case the couple did not divorce, and because I had presided over the woman's conversion and then officiated at their wedding, the three of us were able to sit down and talk. The husband made a concerted effort to be more involved Jewishly in the household. There are far too many other situations that do not have a happy ending.

But assuming that one or both partners, despite all sincere efforts at accommodating each other, remain unyielding in their positions, what then? When all else fails, the only practical solution may be an agreement to fashion a dual family setting in which more than one faith is being practiced by parents and children.

Although far from ideal, this is no longer an unusual situation. There are a growing number of blended families in which children of separate faiths now live together in the same household and where their newly married parents make a concerted effort to maintain each child's respective religious identity.

While it can be argued that the cooperation of parents who are happily married is not comparable to the tensions and struggles for control by divorced parents seeking to indoctrinate a child in a particular faith, the existence of such family arrangements is proof that they can, if necessary, be implemented.

Consultation with an expert in child development who can suggest ways to help children adjust to diverse religious orientations as they move from one household to another is recommended. Both parents will of course have to abide by the consultant's guidelines if the transitions are to be workable

The common sense of parents in these deliberations is also basic. If the two religions being considered are not merely inconsistent with one another, but seek to demean or undermine the other faith, there is no way that a compromise of this kind is feasible.

That was precisely what occurred in a case involving a Jewish woman who had become strictly Orthodox and her former husband who was now a born-again Christian, choices each had made while they were still married to each other and that had led to their divorce.

In a struggle that was finally adjudicated by the Massachusetts Supreme Judicial Court, the mother complained that when the children were with their father, he had cut off the little boy's *payes* and threatened to do the same to the fringes on his *tallit katan*.

He also took both children to a church that taught that those who do not accept its teachings are damned and will go to hell. The father in his court testimony stated that he "would never stop trying to save his children."[10] One can only conjecture about the long-term psychological price these children will pay in the future. It is a sobering reminder of what parents should not do.

There is no way of predicting what effect any of these arrangements will have upon a child's choice of religious identity or well-being in adulthood. Still, parental cooperation and/or consultation with a child development professional, whatever their limitations, remain preferable alternatives to that of a bitter court battle, which can only alienate children further and certainly never accomplish what either parent professes to be doing in their child's best interest.

In defining a child's Jewish identity, it bears repeating that according to Jewish law, a child whose mother is not Jewish either by birth or by choice, though reared as a Jew, is not considered Jewish by Orthodox and Conservative Judaism without a formal conversion performed in accordance with halachic requirements. Only Reform Judaism has embraced the principle of gender neutrality in defining the Jewish status of a child, that is, a child has a presumption of Jewishness at birth if either father or mother is Jewish. The other branches of Judaism continue to define Jewish identity as matrilineal.

There is no indication that these circumstances will change in the foreseeable future. Until they do, children born of an interfaith marriage in which the father is Jewish and the mother is not will not be considered Jewish in Orthodox and Conservative circles. As a result, they will not be permitted to have a bar or bat mitzvah in a non-Reform synagogue or as adults have their marriage to born Jews solemnized by a non-Reform rabbi without undergoing a formal conversion to Judaism.[11]

Even though the controversy over what constitutes Jewish identity has far broader implications than those related to the divorce of interfaith couples, it is an added factor to be reckoned with in this arena. It is not inconceivable that a Jewish father, having succeeded in having his non-Jewish wife agree to their child's upbringing as a Jew, will then discover that, with the exception of Reform Judaism, the child is not classified as Jewish.

Not all intermarriages are destined to end in divorce, nor are all pledges to rear children as Jews broken should a marriage falter. But differences in religious and cultural values should not be minimized or overlooked at any time in the course of a couple's relationship, least of all before determining to marry. Doing so can only set the stage for some version of one of the unhappy scenarios described here.

7 "RABBI, I'M GETTING DIVORCED.

DO I NEED A GET?"

A key unresolved ideological dispute affecting the various branches of Judaism in the United States is the need for and the nature of a Jewish divorce, or get. Where once the issue was the sole concern of Orthodox and Conservative Jews, the matter is now of relevance to Reform Jews as well, as the rate of divorce among Jews rises and second marriages between persons from diverse Jewish backgrounds become more common. Because of its complexity, some historic background about the get may be helpful.

As long as marriage and divorce were governed by Jewish law, the requirement of a get was strictly enforced. A woman who sought to remarry without it was considered to be still married to her first husband, and no rabbi would agree to officiate at a subsequent Jewish ceremony. A second marriage without a get, however valid from a secular point of view, was deemed an act of adultery halachically. Any children born of the relationship were classified as illegitimate, or *mamzerim* in Hebrew.

The latter were subject to severe disabilities. For example, Deut. 23:3 forbade them "to enter the congregation of the Lord even unto the tenth generation." In effect, the ban was a form of permanent social isolation. A *mamzer* could marry only another man or woman who was in the same category. The only other alternative was to leave their community and move to a locale where their backgrounds were unknown and to hope that they would remain that way. Undoubtedly, countless men and women did precisely that over the years.

THE LANGER CASE

The plight of the *mamzer* remains a reality in traditional circles In 1972, an Israeli brother and sister, Hanoch and Miriam Langer, each applied for a marriage license. Both applications were rejected by the Israeli rabbinate on the grounds that the Langer siblings were illegitimate and therefore forbidden to marry "kosher Jews." Apparently, when the Langer children went before the rabbbinical court, a series of questions were raised regarding their mother's marital history in pre-Nazi Poland and her subsequent divorce and remarriage in Israel.

It appeared that Mrs. Langer's past indicated that she had not abided by the requisite halachic standards in her personal relationships. An added complication was the fact that all of her personal records had been lost during World War II. After a much publicized trial before a rabbinical court, and a furor in Israel and in many other places, the court rescinded its original decision. The Langer children were granted full status as Jews, and the marriage licenses were issued.[1] This concern over the possible challenge to the legitimacy of children is a key factor in the renewed interest in the get.

The requirement that a woman's first husband must issue her a get before she may remarry is still binding in Orthodox and Conservative Judaism. The wording of an Orthodox get, "Behold you are now permitted to any man," is most significant. There is no comparable declaration on the part of the woman, who cannot initiate the proceedings for a get. She is still dependent upon her husband to do so. By and large, the Orthodox woman has remained at the mercy of her husband when it comes to a divorce.

Historically, Jewish courts could and did exert pressure on husbands who refused to give their wives a get. These included social isolation, public humiliation, and even physical beatings. This vignette taken from the ruling of an eighteenth-century rabbinical court in Minsk, Russia, is illustrative of what could be and was done to coerce a stubborn husband into giving his wife a get:

a. The contumacious one shall forfeit his rights to participate in Kahal activities or in those of the association.

b. He shall not be called to the reading of the Torah nor shall he be honored with the privilege of performing any ceremony or ritual.

c. He shall not be invited to ceremonial feasts or public celebrations and none shall participate in a feast given by the defiant.

d. No one shall rent an apartment or store from him nor lease any to him.

e. If he be an artisan, it shall be strictly forbidden on penalty of the ban to order work."[2]

But regardless of what a Jewish court may try to do, if a husband persists in his refusal to give his wife a get, the Orthodox woman has no recourse whatsoever. Women in this situation are known as agunot, or chained, and may never remarry. They face a similar problem should their husband desert them and not be found or if he is reported missing or killed and there are no witnesses to his demise.

Because of their dissatisfaction with the Orthodox get and its subordination of a woman's wishes regarding divorce to those of her husband, both the Conservative and Reconstructionist movements have established procedures of their own for securing a get that are sensitive to women's rights. The Conservative movement has added a special clause to its *ketubah* that in effect nullifies a wife's dependence upon her husband for a get.

Known as the Lieberman Clause, in honor of its author, the late professor Saul Lieberman of the Jewish Theological Seminary, it reads:

> As evidence of our desire to enable each other to live in accordance with the Jewish Law of Marriage throughout our lifetime, we the bride and the bridegroom, attach our signature to this Ketubah and hereby agree to recognize the Bet Din of the Rabbinical Assembly of America, or its duly appointed representatives, as having authority to counsel us in light of Jewish tradition which requires husband and wife to give each other complete love and devotion and to summon either party at the request of the other in order to enable the party so requesting to live in accordance with the standards of the Jewish Law of Marriage throughout his or her lifetime. We authorize the Bet Din to impose such terms of compensation as it may see fit for failure to respond to its summons or to carry out its decisions.[3]

The phraseology of the *ketubah* gives the Conservative *beit din* the power to act on behalf of the woman and award her a get even if the husband balks at doing so. The validity of this clause in the Conservative get was tested in the civil courts of New York by a woman named Susan Avitzur, who filed a suit against her husband in 1983.

Her husband had refused to give her a get even though the Conservative *ketubah* they had both signed prior to their marriage had provided for that contingency. In her suit, she argued that his refusal was a violation of what the *ketubah* as a contract required. In upholding her petition, the New York Court of Appeals stated that the *ketubah* was deserving of the same dignity "given any other civil contract that required submission of a dispute to a non-judicial forum."[4] The Reconstructionists not only allow a woman to initiate a divorce proceeding, but also include women as members of the *beit din*.

Orthodox Judaism, which has steadfastly refused to recognize the validity of either the Conservative or the Reconstructionist get, has yet to revise its own proceedings to respond to the needs of women. Repeated pleas to do so have fallen on deaf ears. There are also documented instances when unscrupulous husbands have demanded that their wives pay them exorbitant amounts of money in return for a get.

In a notable exception to Orthodoxy's reluctance to modify its stance regarding women, Orthodox Jewish groups in the state of New York, in 1983, successfully lobbied the New York state legislature to pass a statute that became known as the Get Law. In effect, the law required all plaintiffs in a divorce to declare in a sworn statement that he or she has taken "all steps to remove any barrier to the defendant's remarriage following an annulment or a divorce."[5]

The law was designed to provide Orthodox Jewish women with a means of compelling their husbands to give them a get. Non-Orthodox couples and those with no religious affiliation who were married in Jewish ceremonies without a *ketubah* were exempt from the law. Since the law's passage over a decade ago, there has been little research regarding its impact upon the ability of Orthodox Jewish women to file successfully for divorce.

One critic has pointed to the fact that the law as written makes no provision for persons initially married in a civil ceremony who then become religious and want a get. There is also no provision in the law for someone who first receives a civil divorce and only afterward wants a get.[6] New York is the only state to have passed a law of this kind. However, other states have upheld the validity of a wife's petition to force her husband to give her a get should he refuse to do so.

REFORM JUDAISM AND DIVORCE

Historically, Reform Judaism categorized divorce as a civil matter. The *ketubah,* the get, and the rabbinical court were all eliminated as a part of an effort to break with practices the Reform movement found demeaning to women as well as outdated and irrelevant for Jews living in the modern world. It was also a means of ending Orthodox domination of Jewish life and more fully integrating adherents of Reform Judaism into Western culture.

By these actions, the early Reformers, as they were known, also sought, once and for all, to repudiate charges made during the eighteenth and nineteenth centuries in Europe, that Jews were so clannish, unreliable, and dishonest by nature that they were inherently incapable of becoming full citizens of the countries in which they lived. These allegations were so deeply rooted in European society that even the most ardent champions and advocates of Jews felt obliged to echo them as they pleaded for the full emancipation of Jews. Granted their validity, they said, these deficits were not inherent in Jews, but were caused by social conditions. Give the Jews full equality and they would demonstrate their loyalty and patriotism.[7]

A notable example of the problem is the fact that as late as the middle of the nineteenth-century, substantial numbers of French Jews, particularly those who had moved to France from Eastern Europe, were being married in Jewish ceremonies without bothering to register their marriages with the French civil authorities. The practice was a source of great concern to the leadership of the French Jewish community, who wanted nothing to jeopardize their full integration into French society.[8]

Similar fears may account for the actions taken by the Reform rabbinate in the United States when essentially removing divorce entirely from the religious sphere. In 1929, the Executive Board of the CCAR declared, "When the rabbi officiates at a marriage, he does so as an officer of the state. But a divorce is purely a legal action with which the rabbi has no connection."[9]

The early Reformers may well have believed that ultimately all branches of Judaism flourishing in an open society would give up the halachic requirements for divorce and rely entirely upon the civil courts or that in time a set of common religious procedures for ending a marriage would evolve.

The prospect that Reform Judaism would become the dominant Jewish religious movement in America and that the survival of Orthodoxy was problematic at best, and certainly would never flourish, was another possible explanation for what was done. There may have even been the assumption that Reform Jews would only marry and divorce each other and voluntary segregate themselves from the rest of the Jewish community. In any event, the contemporary patterns of marriage and divorce among Jews in America could simply not have been foreseen.

In the present chaotic situation, the various branches of Judaism have each established their own procedures for granting a get or, in the case of Reform, none at all. Unfortunately, the prospects for working out a mutually acceptable format for dealing with divorce in the Jewish community at any time in the near future are quite remote.

Nor could the spiritual needs of the present generation of Reform Jews be anticipated by the early Reformers. Many Reform Jews are eager to ritualize every aspect of the Jewish life-cycle. They want to do so in ways totally distinct from what the classical Reformers could have imagined and would have found utterly contrary to their aspirations for Jewish observance and religious practice in America.

The demography of the Reform Jewish community in America has been totally transformed in the past 100 years and bears no resemblance whatsoever to its nineteenth-century antecedents. Its religious needs and values reflect that change. In a radical departure from classical Reform's attitude toward divorce as a purely civil matter, the CCAR in 1988 introduced a "Ritual of Release," or *Seder Preidah,* for divorcing couples.

Its intent has been to foster a spiritual setting for the termination of a marriage, thereby hopefully lessening its adversarial potential as well as providing a religious context for the expression of grief and loss. It is not meant to be a Reform version of the get.

Just as the rituals attendant to a Jewish marriage add a unique dimension to what is basically a secular, legal arrangement that could be validated in a wholly civil setting, *Seder Preidah* attempts to create a sacred space and time for making the difficult transition from marriage to singleness. It offers the possibility for healing in spiritual surroundings, precisely at a time when persons are preoccupied with lawyers and courtrooms. It makes tangible the hope expressed in the daily worship service: "Heal us, O Lord, and we shall be healed; save us and we shall be saved; grant us a perfect healing from all our wounds. Blessed is the Lord, the Healer of the sick."[10]

Seder Preidah anticipates a time when divorcing couples will echo the sentiments of Jewish couples who when marrying say, "I wouldn't feel married without a rabbi." Divorcing couples will say, "I wouldn't feel divorced without *Seder Preidah.*"

The very recognition that a special ceremony has been introduced on their behalf may help overcome the sense of so many divorced men and women that they are no longer welcome in the synagogue. Its availability as a ritual may also alleviate the tendency of the divorced to see themselves as failures, an all too familiar state of affairs.

Seder Preidah may not be suitable for every divorcing couple. For some, the ceremony may be too painful; the wounds may still be too raw. For others, the circumstances surrounding the divorce may be too bitter. Yet death is also painful and bitter but is still ritualized even among the least observant.

Although *Seder Preidah* has been a part of Reform Jewish practice for over a decade, not enough people are aware that the ritual exists. Little effort has been made by rabbis to either explain or encourage it. To be sure, rabbis need to feel comfortable in sharing the experience. If they are not, their ambivalence will be easily conveyed to divorcing couples. Those who do participate will find that it offers the closure and the consolation that the various rituals of mourning are meant to offer upon the death of a loved one.

Eli and Tania were a couple at whose wedding I had officiated. I had not heard from them in over ten years when they called to say that they were divorcing and wondered if there was an appropriate Jewish ceremony for them to share. They were not interested, they said, in a get. Tania in particular was prepared to face the consequences of not having one. "I'll cross that bridge if and when I have to," she said to me over the phone.

When we met together, they made it clear that the divorce was necessary. There was no possibility of a reconciliation. They had agreed to a fair and equitable settlement. What they wanted was a religious setting in which to say goodbye.

Getting divorced was hard enough, they said, without having to formalize it solely in a cold, impersonal, and strange courtroom. We reviewed the text of *Seder Preidah*. It was exactly what they were looking for.

A few days later we met in the sanctuary of a local synagogue. The three of us stood before the open ark. As the ritual proceeded, they both wept. I did too. At the end they held each other, and then I held each of them. They left the sanctuary separately, symbolic of beginning independent lives. Later they each sent me a note telling me how meaningful those few moments had been.

It is important that couples understand that this ceremony is not the equivalent of a get and was never intended as such.

Divorcing individuals as well as rabbis should be wary of unscrupulous husbands who for reasons of revenge may attempt to falsely use *Seder Preidah* as a substitute for giving their wives an Orthodox get. Some time prior to the formal introduction of *Seder Preidah*, when individual Reform rabbis who believed in the value of this ritual were still preparing their own ceremonies, I was called upon to testify in a probate court regarding what turned out to be a fraudulent attempt to have a Reform service of separation pass for a get.

A gentleman whose Orthodox ex-wife needed a get in order to remarry deliberately misled a Reform rabbi whom he went to see and from whom he requested some form of symbolic document of release from their marriage.

His wife, he told the rabbi, was totally disinterested in the matter. It was he, he lied, who wanted a religious confirmation of their divorce and wondered if the rabbi could help. The rabbi was very sympathetic and provided a special document that he had composed precisely for this purpose.

The man then doctored the form so that it resembled a get and sent it to his wife, knowing all the while that it would never be accepted by an Orthodox rabbinical court and that as a consequence his former wife would be unable to remarry. She, in turn, sent it to her attorney.

The wife's attorney, who was Jewishly knowledgeable, contacted me and asked when Reform Judaism had begun to grant a get. I replied that I had no idea what she was talking about, since there was no such document. Upon receiving a copy of what her client had sent her, I informed her that it was a forgery. The matter went to court, where after appropriate testimony, the judge ordered the man to grant his wife a genuine Orthodox get within a prescribed period of time or face a contempt of court charge.

A Reform Jewish woman with only a civil divorce should remember that she may have to seek a get from her former husband if her fiancé wishes them to be married by a non-Reform rabbi. There are some Orthodox rabbis who will say that a get is not necessary, since there may be some question about the halachic validity of the woman's first marriage, depending upon who the witnesses to the marriage were. But that is not a universal opinion and should not be relied upon without consultation with a rabbi.

In opting for a get and being compelled to contact one's former husband, the reopening of old wounds and the reawakening of bitter memories are always a possibility. Having to choose between two unappealing alternatives— possible rejection by an Orthodox or Conservative suitor, or having to relive the past in order to secure a happy future—will not be pleasant.

Jewish husbands who are contacted by their former wives need to be cooperative and understanding rather than make the process any more difficult than it already is. The temptation to be stubborn or sarcastic, or even to refuse, is very real.

The Jewish ideal of *derech eretz*, of decency and goodwill and of doing the right thing, ought to be the prevailing sentiment should this occasion arise.

Decisions regarding a get should only be made after a good deal of soul searching has taken place. Prior consultation with a rabbi from the particular branch of Judaism whose *beit din* will preside over the get is also recommended so that the details can be explained and the procedures clarified. Since 1985, an organization called Kayama has been in existence in Brooklyn, New York, for the purpose of counseling women who wish to go through the get process but are fearful or ignorant of what it entails.

To help expand the general Jewish community's awareness of Kayama's objectives, the organization sought the assistance of the CCAR. In response, in 1997, Rabbi Richard Levy, then president of the CCAR, wrote this letter to its entire membership:

> Dear Colleague: Enclosed is a letter from Isaac Skolnik, director of Kayama, an organization dedicated to protecting the rights of Jews who wish to remarry, by assisting them in obtaining a get at the time they obtain a civil divorce. As you know, a Jewish man or woman who is civilly divorced but has not obtained a get may be prevented from marrying by rabbis who require a get. Whatever our own view of gittin may be, to refer couples to Kayama is to preserve their freedom to choose their future spouses and *mesadrei kiddushin* [the rabbi who will officiate at the wedding]. I hope you will read the enclosed material carefully and begin to refer divorced or divorcing couples to the understanding and sensitive people at Kayama.[11]

Unfortunately, there is little hope at the present time that the chaotic nature of Jewish divorce will be remedied in the near future. No discussions are being held among rabbinic representatives of the three major branches of Judaism in the United States for the purpose of developing a common approach to the problem nor are any anticipated. Efforts in the State of Israel to address the plight of literally thousands of Jewish women who cannot remarry either because their husbands refuse to give them a get or because they are *agunot* are essentially at a standstill.

Even when husbands agree to a get, some women may find the experience of appearing before an Orthodox rabbinical court to be humiliating. A woman named Barbara Bialick expressed her feelings in a poem written after undergoing the experience. It is both bitter and poignant.

> There are only three things you need to know about a Jewish divorce. One, this is the real divorce even if your husband doesn't believe it and your friends never heard of it. Two, this is the real divorce even if your mother makes you do it. Three, the civil divorce is irrelevant to God.

> There's one part you won't remember. It's the part when your husband is allowing you your freedom. What are you anyway that you can be given away? Silently you will thank them for

protecting the legitimacy of children you don't plan to have....
At the end the rabbis will presume they did you a mitzvah.
Better luck next time, Basha Ruchel.[12]

In recent years, an increasing number of creative divorce rituals for both men and women have been written. None of them have halachic standing and are not intended as such. But they can be comforting and uplifting. They are included here along with the text of *Seder Preidah* and examples of traditional documents of marriage and divorce and related matters.

RABBI VICKI HOLLANDER'S DOCUMENT OF TRANSITION

Vicki Hollander, an ordained Reform rabbi, who went through an Orthodox Get, prepared an additional ritual for herself and her husband. The night before their appearance before the Bet Din, she composed her own personal Document of Transition which she signed and would hand to her husband upon the receipt of their Get. The morning of the Bet Din she recited the Viddui, the Confessional, which Jews recite when they are about to die. She dressed in white and put on a Talit.

The Document of Transition contained the following declaration:

"This day I am no longer bound to the task and to the commitment to cherish and honor you in faithfulness and in integrity as my husband.

This day I am no longer bound to stand as wife, companion, and partner.

This day I am no longer bound by honor or by law to affirm and maintain kedusha within our relationship. This day I am no longer set aside, special to only you. This day the kedusha vows become null and void. I am no longer bound by the vows of kedushin. Hereby, I am no longer kedusha to you, no longer your wife and you are no longer kadosh to me, no longer my husband.

On this day according to our tradition I depart as a free woman.

I stand as a free agent in the Jewish community, in the world and before myself.

I stand having completed our people's traditional way of unbinding a marital relationship.

I stand as a Jewish woman with dignity and with strength.

I stand restored to a single unit as a whole and complete person.

This shall stand as a document of release and a letter of freedom in accordance with the values of our people Israel."

After she and her now former husband received their Get, she returned home, bathed and put on comfortable, colored clothes and new colored earrings which she had bought for this occasion. Women friends came to the house bringing food and refreshments. Together they said the Blessing of Shehechiyanu and then walked around the block, again symbolic of what mourners do upon the completion of the Sheva, the seven days of mourning after a loved one's death.[13]

A *HAVDALAH* RITUAL FOR WHEN A MARRIAGE COMES APART

(A Ceremony Created by a Rosh Hodesh Group of Princeton, New Jersey)

Naomi, one member of our Jewish women's group asked us for a ceremony to mark her separation from her husband, Joseph. Naomi and Joseph [their names have been changed here] had been married for nineteen years, and in the past several years conflicts between them had escalated to the point where Naomi felt that it was not possible for her to continue in the marriage....

Ultimately, though our ceremony was held on a Sunday evening, we chose to use and reinterpret the symbols of *Havdalah*...to enable Naomi to mark this transition to a new phase of her life.

About twelve of us gathered in a living room to conduct the ceremony, which took about an hour and a half....

We began with an abbreviated *Ma'ariv* (Evening) service... We used the new Reconstructionist prayer book,... from which we selected readings... The readings introduced the themes of endings, separation, and death, setting the tone for the ceremony that followed.

We sang a simple *niggun*,... a kind of comforting lullaby when sung softly and slowly.

Lighting two candles, we poured wine for all, and recited three blessings together:

> *We praise You, Source of Life, for the wine that helps heal our wounds and points to future joys. (We drank the wine.)*

> *We praise You, Source of Life, for the fragrance that enables us to savor pleasant memories of shared experiences. (We pass around the fragrant wood chips.)*

> *We praise You, Source of Life, for the flame that lights the direction to the future, guiding us to new paths. (The flames of the two candles were held together for the blessing, and separated afterward.)*

Naomi then read these blessings aloud:

> *Blessed is the One who separates and makes distinctions.*

> *Blessed is the One who guided me to join my husband under the huppah [marriage canopy].*

> *Blessed is the One who enabled us to bring our children into the world.*

> *Blessed is the One who sheltered us in our home.*

> *Blessed is the One who has helped me to decide to leave this marriage.*

Blessed is the One who separates and makes distinctions....

We wanted to give Naomi an opportunity to talk about her marriage, to tell its story to the group and to herself....

Question Prompts:

- when you met—what was/is attraction
- courtship and decision to marry
- wedding/early years/birth of children
- moment(s) of greatest joy/sadness
- what has made you most angry
- regret—what you feel you could have done differently
- Jewish life
- turning points—looking back, when were they?
- how have you changed since the beginning of this relationship?
- what do you know now that you wish you had known then?
- other questions...

I had earlier asked Naomi to bring something symbolizing her marriage to burn. She brought a copy of her marriage license.... She placed it in a bowl, along with the fragrant wood chips,... and lit them with both of the candles.... While everything was burning, Naomi repeated this passage below phrase by phrase after me:

I, Naomi S., affirm that I have chosen, with sorrow and with anger, with regret and with relief, to end my marriage to Joseph B. Before we were joined; as of now, we are separated. Before, we shared our home; now, we live in separate homes. I leave behind me forever my married life with Joseph. I look ahead to a new life for myself, a life that will grow from the sweetness and the bitterness of our marriage.

Blessed is the One who separates and makes distinctions.

Blessed is the One who enables us to make transformations and new beginnings.

97

We mixed the ashes of the marriage certificate and the wood chips with potting soil and the objects in the pot, and we then placed the plant into the soil....

We ended by chanting our opening *niggun*.... We all stood in a close circle, with Naomi in the middle.... we found ourselves growing quiet, hugging and slowly rocking Naomi as a group. We gradually stepped back from her, and she hugged each of us individually.... We lingered in the spell of the moment, all of us bound together by the moving experience we had shared.[14]

A MEDITATION UPON LEAVING THE MARITAL RESIDENCE

Often a divorce necessitates that the family residence be sold. This can be a particularly painful experience for all concerned. Even though there is a ceremony of consecration for a new home, there is no ritual of farewell when leaving one's previous home, regardless of the circumstances surrounding the move. But when the move is a consequence of divorce, emotions can be especially raw. This suggested meditation can be recited as a family or individually. Either way, it may provide some needed comfort.

O God, who daily renews the work of creation, grant me the courage to carry on, the wisdom to learn from adversity, and the strength to rebuild my life. I am grateful for the years of joy and fulfillment that were mine within these walls. The pain of leaving is eased by memories I shall carry with me and the resolve to fashion another abode where Your presence will prevail. Trusting in You, I shall again affix a mezuzah to the doorpost of my new home, ever mindful that unless You build the house, those who build it labor in vain.

SEDER PREIDAH: RITUAL OF RELEASE

Rabbi: Since earliest times Judaism has provided for divorce when a woman and a man, who have been joined together in *kiddushin* (sacred matrimony), no longer experience the sacred in their relationship. The decision to separate is painful, not only for the woman and the man (and for their children), but for the entire community. Jewish tradition teaches that when the sacred covenant of marriage is dissolved, "even the altar sheds tears." (Gitin 90b)

W, have you consented to the termination of your marriage?

(*W responds.*)

M, have you consented to the termination of your marriage?

(*M responds.*)

W: I, _____, now release my former husband, _____, from the sacred bonds that held us together.

M: I, _____, now release my former wife, _____, from the sacred bonds that held us together.

Rabbi: W and M, _____ years ago you entered into the covenant of *kiddushin.* Now you have asked us to witness your willingness to release each other from the sacred bond of marriage, and your intention to enter a new phase of life.

What existed between you, both the good and the bad, is ingrained in your memories. We pray that the good that once existed between you may encourage you to treat each other with respect and trust, and to refrain from acts of hostility. (And may the love that you have for your children, and the love that they have for you, increase with years and understanding.)

(*Personal words by rabbi.*)

This is your Document of Separation, duly signed by you both. It marks the dissolution of your marriage. I separate it now as you have separated, giving each of you a part.

W and M, you are both now free to enter into a new phase of

your life. Take with you the assurance that human love and sanctity endure.

May God watch over each of you and protect you as you go your separate ways.

And let us say: Amen.

Document of Separation

On _____, the _____ day of _____, in the year 57_____ (the _____ day of _____, in the year _____of the civil calendar), according to the calendar that we use here in the city of _____, state of _____—I, _____, release my former husband,_____, from the sacred bonds that held us together. He is free and responsible for his life, just as I am free and responsible for my life. This is his Document of Separation from me.[15]

(The Document of Separation whereby the husband releases his wife is the same except for the gender references.)

THE ORTHODOX GET

The Get is handwritten on an unattached paper by a Sofer [a scribe], who writes in Torah script with a special quill pen. It consists of twelve lines of writing and must be signed by two witnesses who also write in Torah script. The twelve lines of writing correspond to the twelve prescribed lines of empty space that separate the first four books of the Torah. The purpose of these specifications is to teach us that a Get given in accordance with Jewish law is one of the 613 commandments, hence it is an act of holiness.

Composition of the Get

Every Get must contain five things:

1. The statement that the husband divorces the wife....

2. The statement that once the Get is granted, there is absolutely no further relationship between the husband and the wife.

3. The time and place of the writing of the Get.

4. The Get must be written for the wife and must specify all the names by which she is known in Hebrew and in English (except her family name); her Jewish name, and her father's Hebrew and English name, and his designation as being a Kohen or a Levi.

5. The Get must be written on unattached paper so that when completed it is a self-contained document and can immediately be presented to the wife.

Once the Get has been given, each party receives a document from the Beth Din certifying that the marriage has been legally dissolved.

The Text of the Get Written in Aramaic

On the _____ day of the week, in the _____ month of the year _____ of the creation of the universe according to our count in this city of _____ which has a _____ (river) or is located on _____ (ocean)

I, _____ (Husband's name) son of _____ Kohen or Levi, who is standing here in _____ (city) with _____ (river) of my own free will without being compelled to do so, declare my intention to divorce and free you, my wife,_____ (wife's name) daughter of _____, Kohen or Levi, who is standing here in _____ (city) with _____ (river). You who have been my wife from before, I free and release you, so that you can marry anyone you wish, and no one can prohibit you from doing this. Today and forever you are free to marry any man. This will be in your hands a book of divorce and a document of freedom according to the law of Moses and Israel.

_____witness

_____witness

THE HALACHIC GROUNDS FOR DIVORCE

1. Mutual agreement by both parties

2. Huband's grounds

   a. Adultery committed by wife; suspicion of adultery.

   b. Public behavior flouting the laws of modesty.

   c. Wife's apostasy from Judaism or such disregard of Jewish law as to cause the husband to transgress as well.

   d. Refusal for one year by wife to allow the husband his conjugal rights.

   e. Refusal of wife to allow the husband to move to the dwelling place he had clearly designated at the time of the wedding; or to follow him to the land of Israel or to Jerusalem.

   f. Wife suffers from incurable diseases that make cohabitation impossible or dangerous, and from mental illnesses which, while not incapacitating her for legal acts, render bleak the prospects for domestic peace.

   g. Wife's incapacity to bear children.

3. Wife's grounds

   a. Husband contracted a loathsome chronic disease after marriage.

   b. Husband, after the marriage, engaged in a vocation that made him disgusting to his spouse so as to make cohabitation impossible.

   c. Repeated cruel treatment by the husband.

   Husband's apostasy from Judaism.

   d. Husband's squandering his property and refusing to support his wife.

   e. Husband committed an offense that forced him to flee the country.

   f. Husband's sterility or impotence (admitted by him) in a

situation in which the wife claims that she desires children as a support and comfort for her in her later years.

g. Husband's persistent refusal to engage in sexual intercourse with his wife.

h. Husband consorts habitually with prostitutes.

4. Grounds invoked by the Court against the will of both parties

a. Where marriage, though forbidden in Biblical or Rabbinic law, is binding as a fait accompli.

b. Where the husband is willing to continue the marriage relationship though the wife is guilty of adultery.

ch. Where considerations of hygiene forbid sexual intercourse, divorce is not enforced if the parties consent to marriage without cohabitation.[16]

MODEL TRADITIONAL *KETUBAH*

On the (first) day of the week, the day of the month in the year five thousand six hundred and since the creation of the world, the era according to us which we are accustomed to reckon here in city of (name of city, state and country) (name of bridegroom) son of (name of father) surnamed (family name), said to this virgin (name of bride), daughter of (name of father) surnamed (family name): "Be thou my wife according to the law of Moses and Israel, and I will cherish, honor, support and maintain thee in accordance with the custom of Jewish husbands who cherish, honor, support and maintain their wives in truth. And I herewith make for thee the settlement of virgins, two hundred silver zuzim, which belongs to thee, according to the law of Moses and Israel; and (I will also give thee) thy food, clothing and necessaries, and live with thee as husband and wife according to universal custom."

And Miss (name of bride) consented and became his wife. The

wedding outfit that she brought unto him from her father's house, in silver, gold, valuables, wearing apparel, house furniture and bedclothes, all this (name of bridegroom) accepted in the sum of one hundred silver pieces. And the bridegroom consented to increase this amount from his own property with the sum of one hundred silver pieces making in all two hundred silver pieces. And thus said the bridegroom: "The responsibility of this marriage contract, of this wedding outfit, and of this additional sum, I take upon myself and my heirs after me, so that they shall be paid from the best part of my property and possession that I have beneath the whole heaven, that which I now possess or may hereafter acquire.

"All my property, real and personal, even the mantle on my shoulders, shall be mortgaged to secure the payment of this marriage contract, of the wedding outfit and of the addition made thereto, during my lifetime and after my death from the present day and forever." The bridegroom has taken upon himself the responsibility of this marriage contract, of the wedding outfit and the additions made thereto, according to the restrictive usages of all marriage contracts and the additions thereto made for the daughters of Israel, in accordance with the institutions of our sages of blessed memory.[17]

8 IN CONCLUSION

This guide has been written to better acquaint readers with the many facets of divorce from a contemporary Jewish perspective. Its emphasis has been upon the spiritual, in the belief that approaching divorce within a Jewish religious frame of reference will exert a positive influence on how its legal aspects are resolved and can help uncover untapped inner resources that can be so vital during this trying period.

While intended for those going through this ordeal, it also is directed to a wider audience. Rabbis, synagogue educators, and Jewish family agency professionals may find it helpful in their work with an increasingly large segment of the Jewish community, not to mention the general reader, who more often than not has numerous misconceptions about Judaism and divorce and may find its contents enlightening.

Divorcing without malice is not an ideal that is limited to a single religious or ethnic group. The book's Jewish focus notwithstanding, much of what is recommended in these pages may be of value to anyone who is divorcing, whatever their religious beliefs.

Certain divorce issues, such as the distribution of property, pensions, and other assets, estate planning, and taxes, have either been omitted entirely or only briefly touched upon. These are highly complex matters demanding an intimate knowledge of tax and real estate law as well as other legal nuances.

Their clarification is also dependent upon the specific histories of the parties to whom they apply, as well as the requirements of the jurisdictions where they reside. Nor is a detailed discussion of them the purpose of this work. Information regarding these subjects can be found elsewhere.

Critics may argue that publishing a guide for divorcing couples is a way of tacitly condoning the breakdown of the Jewish family and is therefore inappropriate, especially at a time when the Jewish family is in disarray.

Such reactions are both unfortunate and quite shortsighted. No faith community, least of all Judaism, serves its adherents very effectively by denying reality.

Pretending that divorce does not exist will not make it disappear. Withholding publications that discuss it openly can only worsen the plight of those involved in it. Pressuring couples to stay together regardless of circumstances is not only inconsistent with Jewish tradition, but can only guarantee the continuing misery of dysfunctional families and their further alienation from Judaism and from a Jewish community that they already feel does not care about them.

Helping families cope with the pressures of modern society and teaching them how to strengthen their relationships are a commendable and necessary synagogue goal. Some suggested ways of achieving this have been mentioned in these pages. However, engaging in these programs is not an acceptable rationale for avoiding the problems of the divorced and doing nothing to help alleviate them.

On the contrary, demonstrating to couples that there is a powerful Jewish component to ending a marriage and that saying goodbye can be done without relentless antagonism is an equally binding synagogue responsibility. It is unfortunate that over the years as the more regressive features of divorce law in America were revised, Jewish religious bodies were conspicuous by their absence from the debate, despite their often forthright stands on numerous issues of social justice and Judaism's historic and detailed directives regarding divorce.

As a consequence, divorce reform has largely been the initiative of secular groups. Rightly or wrongly, divorcing Jewish couples have interpreted this as a clear message that their problems did not merit the attention of the Jewish community and that they were being told to take their anguish and themselves elsewhere. They perceived that they and their children were less than welcome in the synagogue, which was reserved for intact families, and that somehow their very presence was construed as a threat to the marital well-being of other members.

The message within these pages to synagogues and to Jewish family agencies is that although there is a new awareness of the concerns of the divorced and although more programming than ever before has been implemented, there is more that can be done. Divorce support groups should be encouraged. Greater sensitivity to the financial disabilities of divorced persons is needed when determining the cost of synagogue membership. More enlightened textbooks and religious school curricula that address the issues of divorce and do so con-structively are long overdue.

Efforts from the pulpit to discourage adversarial confrontations should be increased, along with stressing the potential benefits of mediation and other alternatives to litigation. The utilization of *Seder Preidah* and other innovative rituals should be encouraged. In sum, the synagogue should be seen as a safe haven and not as a problematic source of support at a crucial time in one's life.

The message to couples whose relationships are in trouble and who are undecided whether to go their separate ways is simple. Be sure that you have tried with all of your power to work things out. Be neither hasty nor impulsive.

But when there is no other alternative, then do separate.

Where divorce is necessary, let it be done with mutual respect and the memory of what was once shared together. If there are children, remember that the bonds between you will not be severed for a very long time, if ever, and that how you treat one another will affect their lives as well as yours. In taking your leave, let the memories of a shared past and hopes for a brighter future shape all of your actions.

ADDITIONAL READINGS
AND MEDITATIONS

God, You give meaning to our hopes, to our struggles and our strivings. Without You we are lost, our lives empty. And so when all else fails us, we turn to You! In the stillness of night, when the outer darkness enters the soul; in the press of the crowd, when we walk alone though yearning for companionship; and when in agony we are bystanders to our own confusion, we look to You for hope and peace.

God, we do not ask for a life of ease, for happiness without alloy. Instead we ask You to teach us to be uncomplaining and unafraid. In our darkness help us to find Your light, and in our loneliness to discover the many spirits akin to our own. Give us strength to face life with hope and courage, that even from its discords and conflicts we may draw blessing. Make us understand that life calls us not merely to enjoy the richness of the earth, but to exult in heights attained after the toil of climbing.[1]

Do not withhold good from one who deserves it
When you have the power to do it [for him].
Do not say to your fellow, "Come back again;
I'll give it to you tomorrow," when you have it with you.
Do not devise harm against your fellow
Who lives trustfully with you.
Do not quarrel with a man for no cause,
When he had done you no harm.
Do not envy a lawless man,
Or choose any of his ways.

Proverbs 3:27–31

Though I am belittled and despised,
    I have not neglected Your precepts.
Your righteousness is eternal;
    Your teaching is true.
Though anguish and distress come upon me,
    Your commandments are my delight.
Your righteous decrees are eternal;
    give me understanding, that I might live.

Psalm 119:141–144

See my affliction and rescue me,
    for I have not neglected Your teaching.
Champion my cause and redeem me;
    preserve me according to Your promise.

Psalm 119:153–155

Mother/Father God, God of the broken hearted, God of the strong and the weak, God of the angry and the grieving: I stand before You today in pain, in doubt, in fear. Many blessings have been taken from me; I hesitate even to call out to You and yet I must, with every breath, try to speak Your praise, try to be mindful of being alive. O God, thank You for the gift of this breath.[2]

I awake in pain, misery, and utter confusion; but still I awake. My life is sacred. My life has purpose and my soul houses holy spirit. I pray for healing and to heal others. I gratefully acknowledge today with its infinite possibilities and opportunities. And let me say, Amen.[3]

Blessed art Thou…thank You…the warmth of Your love as it courses through my body and soul…and for the ability to recognize and count your blessing…[4]

Dear God: Thanks for providing me with so many rich experiences and helping lead me down a path woven with living friends and family. My fond and grateful memories sustain me during this difficult time. I never feel alone with your guiding presence surrounding me.[5]

Thank you God/ Power for healing forces in the universe to

which we are attuned as we are to the stars, and the moon, and the seasons, and the hours of the day.[6]

Blessed be God, who holds me to Her breast when I am broken and cradles me when my body and spirit ache.[7]

Blessed are you, Eternal God, who has awakened my soul to a new day, allowing me to love and be loved by others.[8]

Blessed are You, God, Creator and Power of the Universe. You have created beauty in the trees, flowers and mountains. Although I am in pain and cannot always see and feel that beauty, I thank You for creating it.[9]

Hal'lu: Praise

Praise the world—
praise its fullness
and its longing,
its beauty and its grief.

Praise stone and fire,
lilac and river,
and the solitary bird
at the window.

Praise the moment
when the whole
bursts through pain

and the moment
when the whole
bursts forth in joy.

Praise the dying beauty
with all your breath
and, praising, see

the beauty of the world
is your own.[10]

Today Is Forever

I stroll in a nearby park—
old trees wildly overgrown,
bushes, flowers blooming all four seasons,...

Leaning on the railing,
looking at myself
in clear water,
I ask Little creek,
will you tumble and flow here forever?
The stream babbles back, laughing:
Today is forever, forever is now....

A calm slips between the trees,
the leaves move barely a breath,
the grasses ever-so-slightly bow,
and I, steeped in silence,
walk slowly home,

a spark's-worth believing,
a sigh's-worth not believing:
Today is forever. Forever is now.[11]

Aleynu L'shabeyah: It Is Ours to Praise

It is ours to praise
the beauty of the world

even as we discern
the torn world.

For nothing is whole
that is not first rent

and out of the torn
we make whole again.

May we live with promise
in creation's lap,

redemption budding
in our hands.[12]

Interpretive Version: Ahavat Olam

We are loved by an unending love.
We are embraced by arms that find us
even when we are hidden from ourselves.

We are touched by fingers that soothe us
even when we are too proud for soothing.
We are counseled by voices that guide us
even when we are too embittered to hear.
We are loved by an unending love.

We are supported by hands that uplift us
even in the midst of a fall.
We are urged on by eyes that meet us
even when we are too weak for meeting.
We are loved by an unending love.

Embraced, touched, soothed and counseled…
ours are the arms, the fingers, the voices;
ours are the hands, the eyes, the smiles;
We are loved by an unending love.

Blessed are you, Beloved One, who loves your people Israel.

Rami M. Shapiro[13]

Introductions to the Amidah

Dear God,
Open the blocked passageways to you,
The congealed places.

Roll away the heavy stone from the well as your servant
Jacob did when he beheld his beloved Rachel.
Help us open the doors of trust that have been jammed with
hurt and rejection.

As you open the blossoms in spring,
Even as you open the heavens in storm,
Open to us—to feel you great, awesome, wonderful presence.

Sheila Peltz Weinberg[14]

Untie

Dear God,
We are bound with very tight knots.
They choke off air and stop the blood from pulsating freely.
The knots make us like computers with carefully controlled
circuitry.
The knots in our brains tie our creativity—our link with You.
We follow the know around in its intricacy—but it remains a
knot.
The knots in our hearts keep us from crying and dancing when
we long to—
They tie us to the posts of the fences that separate us from
each other.
The knots in our muscles keep our teeth clenched, our jaws
locked, our legs crossed, our shoulders stooped, our backs
bent, our chests from inhaling and exhaling the full sweetness
of life's breath.
O, God, untie all our knots!

Sheila Peltz Weinberg[15]

NOTES

Introduction

1.   *National Jewish Population Survey* (New York: Council of Jewish Federations, 1990), 16–18. A problem related to estimating the Jewish divorce rate is the high percentage of remarriages among Jews. A 1987 study of Jewish marital patterns found that 19 percent of all first marriages involving two born Jews ended in divorce. See Barry Kosmin, Nava Lerer, and Egon Mayer, "Intermarriage, Divorce and Remarriage among American Jews, 1982–87," *North American Jewish Data Bank,* August 1989, 1.

2.   "A Statement of Principles for Reform Judaism," adopted by the Central Conference of American Rabbis at the 1999 Pittsburgh Convention, May 1999—Sivan 5759, 5.

3.   The rabbinic discomfort with bachelorhood is also reflected in this statement: "He who reaches the age of twenty and has not married spends all his days in sin. Sin actually? Say better all his days in the thought of sin" (B. *Kiddushin* 39b).

4.   Jacob Fried, Ed., *Jews and Divorce* (New York: KTAV, 1968), 20–21. In Moslem countries, polygamy among Jews continued for many centuries. Some scholars have maintained that the relative paucity of actual divorces mentioned in the Bible may have been due to the institutions of polygamy and concubinage and that, despite its less than savory implications, the system may have enabled those involved to stay married whatever the circumstances. See Fried, 36–37.

5.   Jacob Bazak, *Jewish Law and Jewish Life,* trans. Stephen Passamaneck, bks. 7, 8 (New York: UAHC Press, 1977), 42, 49.

6.   Israel Abrahams, *Jewish Life in the Middle Ages* (New York: Meridian Books, 1958), 116–17.

7.   Fried, *Jews and Divorce,* 57.

8.   Isaac Metzker, *A Bintel Brief: 60 Years of Letters from the Lower East Side to "The Jewish Daily Forward"* (Garden City, N.Y.: Doubleday, 1971), 83–84.

9. Ibid., 57.

10. "Divorce and the Jewish Child," *National Jewish Family Center Newsletter,* summer 1981, 1.

CHAPTER ONE

1. Robert Bellah et al., *Habits of the Heart* (New York: Harper & Row, 1986), 14.

2. Gunhil O. Hagestad, "The Aging Society as a Context for Family Life," *Daedalus,* Winter 1986, 131.

3. "Predicting Whether a Marriage Will Last," *Boston Globe,* 29 December 1996, 18.

CHAPTER TWO

1. *Gates of Prayer for Assemblies* (New York: Central Conference of American Rabbis, 1993), 1.

CHAPTER THREE

1. Jerrald S. Auerbach, *Justice without Law* (New York: Oxford University Press, 1983), 9.

2. Homer Clark, *The Law of Domestic Relations in the United States* (St. Paul: West Publishing, 1961), 242–3.

3. Auerbach, *Justice without Law,* 80.

4. Ibid.

5. Rita Pollak, "Beyond the Code of Professional Responsibility— Can Spiritual Values Be Our Compass?" (paper delivered before Boston Committee on Restorative Justice, October 18, 1997), 4.

6. Pauline H. Tesler, "Collaborative Law: A New Approach to Family Law," *Conflict Management,* Summer 1996, 17.

Chapter Four

1.   See George Foot Moore, *Judaism* (Cambridge: Harvard University Press, 1954), 2:127–28.

2.   Judith Hauptman, *Rereading the Rabbis: A Woman's Voice* (Boulder, Colo.: Westminster Press, 1998), 61–65.

3.   Susan Faludi, *Backlash: The Undeclared War against American Women* (New York: Crown Publishers, 1991), 24.

4.   Sylvia Barack Fishman, "The Changing American Jewish Family in the 80's," *Contemporary Jewry* 9 (fall 1988): 10–11.

5.   For a thorough airing of the whole issue of bar mitzvah and American culture, see Jeffrey Salkin, *Putting God on the Guest List* (Woodstock, Vt.: Jewish Lights, 1995).

6.   Harlene Appelman, "An Honest Look at Remarriage Families" (paper presented at Conference on the Synagogue and the New Jewish Family, HUC-JIR, New York, 1980), 10.

7.   Correspondence between the author and members of the CCAR.

8.   Paul Buser, "The First Generation of Step Children," *Family Law Quarterly* 25, no. 1 (1986): 12.

9.   *Gates of Prayer: The New Union Prayer Book* (New York: Central Conference of American Rabbis, 1975), 333.

10.   These include Julie Ringold Spitzer, *Spousal Abuse in Contemporary Judaism* (New York: National Federations of Temple Sisterhoods, 1985); Ian Russ, Sally Weber, and Ellen Ledley, *Sholom Bayit, A Jewish Response to Child Abuse and Domestic Violence* (Los Angeles: University of Judaism–Jewish Family Service, 1993); Abraham Twerski, *The Shame Borne in Silence: Spousal Abuse and the Jewish Community* (Pittsburgh: Mikvor Publishers, 1996).

11.   Ruth Mason, "Domestic Values in Israel," *The Jewish Woman*, summer 1999, 29.

12.   Rachel Biale, *Women and Jewish Law* (New York: Schocken Books, 1984), 94.

13.   Ibid., 95.

14.   Ibid., 262–64.

Chapter Five

1. *Gates of Prayer: The New Union Prayer Book* (New York: Central Conference of American Rabbis, 1975) 671.

2. Ibid., 672.

Chapter Six

1. *National Jewish Population Survey* (New York: Council of Jewish Federations 1990), 18.

2. Ibid.

3. Statistics gathered by the Intermarriage Research Institute of New York reveal that in 1989 the divorce rate among the mixed married was 50 percent higher than that of the in-married (memorandum sent to the author by Egon Mayer, Institute Director).

4. *Friederwitzer v Friederwitzer,* Index no. 21095/78, New York, Supreme Court Nassau County, 2 October 1980, 3.

5. Attorney Cynthia Green as quoted by Dirk Johnson, "Parents Battle Over Faith," *New York Times,* 11 December 1988, 1, 8.

6. Joan Wexler, "Rethinking the Modification of Child Custody Decrees," *Yale University Law Journal* 94 (March 1985): 757.

7. Marshall S. Zola, letter to author, April 9, 1996.

8. Kenneth H. Ernstoff, "Forcing Rites on Children," *Family Advocate* 6 (winter 1988): 15.

9. Wexler, "Rethinking."

10. See *Kendall v Kendall,* 7 October 1997–9 December 1997, Supreme Judicial Court of Massachusetts, 10.

11. The Principle of Patrilineal Descent reads in part: "This presumption of the Jewish status of the offspring of any mixed marriage is to be established through appropriate and timely public and formal acts of identification with the Jewish faith and people" (*Rabbi's Manual* [New York: Central Conference of American Rabbis, 1988] 226).

CHAPTER SEVEN

1. Alexander Guttmann, *The Struggle over Reform in Rabbinic Literature* (New York: World Union for Progressive Judaism, 1977), 132–36.

2. Calvin Goldscheider and Alan S. Zukerman, *The Transformation of the Jews* (Chicago: University of Chicago Press, 1986), 22–23.

3. See Linda Kahan, "Jewish Divorce and the Promise of Avitzur," *Georgetown Law Journal* 73 (1984): 213.

4. Ibid., 203.

5. Edward S. Nadel, "New York's Get Laws: A Constitutional Analysis," *Columbia Journal of Law and Social Problems* 27 (fall 1993): 99. At the time of the law's passage, it was estimated that 15,000 women living in the state of New York were *agunot*.

6. Ibid., 98.

7. See the writings of Christian Wilhelm Duhm, "Concerning the Amelioration of the Civil Status of the Jews," trans. Helen Lederer, in *Readings in Modern Jewish History,* ed. Ellis Rivkin (Cincinnati: Hebrew Union College, 1957).

8. Phyllis Cohen Albert, *The Modernization of French Jewry: Consistoire and Community in the 19th Century* (Hanover, N.H.: Brandeis University Press, 1977), 146–48.

9. *Rabbi's Manual* (New York: Central Conference of American Rabbis, 1961), 139.

10. *Gates of Prayer: The New Union Prayer Book* (New York: Central Conference of American Rabbis, 1975), 63.

11. *Kayama Newsletter* 2 (fall 1997): 1.

12. Barbara Bialick, "Jewish Divorce," *Lilith,* summer 1986, 31.

13. Vicki Hollander, "The New, Improved Jewish Divorce: Hers/His" *Lilith,* summer 1990, 20–21.

14. Ruth Berger Goldston, "A Havdalah Ritual for when a Marriage Comes Apart," *Lilith,* spring 1993, 28–29.

15. *Rabbi's Manual* (New York: Central Conference of American Rabbis, 1988), 97–104.

16. Jacob Fried, ed. *Jews and Divorce* (New York: KTAV, 1967), 194–95.

17. Hyman E. Goldin, ed., *Hamadrikh: The Rabbi's Guide* (New York: Hebrew Publishing Co., 1939), 17–20.

ADDITIONAL READINGS AND MEDITATIONS

1. *Gates of Prayer for Assemblies* (New York: Central Conference of American Rabbis, 1993), 1.

2. *When the Body Hurts the Soul Still Longs to Sing* (San Francisco: Jewish Healing Center, 1992), 5.

3. Ibid., 6.

4. Ibid., 7.

5. Ibid., 8.

6. Ibid., 9.

7. Ibid.

8. Ibid.

9. Ibid., 11.

10. Marcia Falk, *The Book of Blessings: New Jewish Prayers for Daily Life, the Sabbath, and the New Moon Festival* (Boston: Beacon Press, 1996), 158.

11. Ibid., 220–222.

12. Ibid., 288.

13. *Kol Haneshamah: Shabbat Vehagim* (Wyncote, Penn.: Reconstructionist Press, 1994), 61.

14. Ibid., 88.

15. Ibid., 748.

SUGGESTED READINGS

Aiken, Linda. *To Be a Jewish Woman*. London: Jason Aronson, 1992.

Berman, Claire. *Adult Children of Divorce Speak Out*. New York: Simon and Schuster, 1997.

Galper, Miriam. *Co-Parenting: A Source Book for the Separated and Divorced*. Philadelphia: Running Press, 1978.

Greenberg, Blu. *On Women and Judaism*. Philadelphia: Jewish Publication Society, 1981.

Krementz, Jill. *How It Feels When Parents Divorce*. New York: Alfred A. Knopf, 1988.

Markman, Howard, Scott Stanley, and Susan Blumberg, *Fighting for Your Marriage*. San Francisco: Jossey–Bass, 1994.

Ricci, Isolina. *Mom's House, Dad's House*. New York: Macmillan, 1980.

Rofes, Eric. *The Kid's Book of Divorce*. Lexington, Mass.: Lewis, 1981.

Scarf, Maggie. *Intimate Partners in Love and Marriage*. New York: Random House, 1987.

Viorst, Judith. *Necessary Losses*. New York: Simon and Schuster, 1986.

Weitzman, Lenore. *The Divorce Revolution*. New York: Free Press, 1985